CHINA: THE BIG LIE?

Mario Cavolo

CHINA: THE BIG LIE?

THE TRUTH OF TRILLIONS IN A CULTURE OF CASH

Mario Cavolo

LONG RIVER PRESS
SAN FRANCISCO

ISBN: 978-1-59265-164-1

Published in the United States of America by:
Sinomedia International Group
Long River Press
360 Swift Avenue, Suite 48
South San Francisco, CA 94080
www.chinabooks.com

Cover design: Tiffany Cha
Text Design: Lisa DeSpain

Printed in the U.S.A.

DEDICATION

To my darling wife Nana. I love you more each day.

IN FONDEST MEMORY OF MY FATHER

Mario Frank Cavolo

December 4, 1930 - June 19, 2013

By our efforts and the Grace of God we go.

My Dad did read this manuscript before it was finally published.
And he liked it very much.

Advance Praise for *China: The Big Lie?*

"This book describes life, behavior and money in China in an entirely new light and is a wonderfully engaging account of life and business there. Unexpected brilliant insight into the lives of real people provides the reader a new and fresh perspective to help make sense of reality in China today. A 'must read.'"

Rory Farquhar Thomson
Head of Corporate & Institutional Banking
Intesa Sanpaolo SpA, Shanghai

***

"Cavolo has written the *Freakonomics* for China watchers. What Dubner and Levitt did for our assumptions about how America and the global economy work, he does for China, upending all of our notions of how things are by combining shrewd observation, cultural insight, and basic microeconomics to blow apart finance column clichés about China's rise. A must read for anyone perplexed about how this complicated and frustrating country keeps going—and keeps foiling its critics."

Nicholas MacDonald
Editorial Director, iTV-Asia

***

" . . . packed with spot on, real life stories that deliver unexpected insights into the real world of a rising China and across the world. This book delivers a discerning, entertaining scope that sheds much needed light both essential and entertaining."

David Turchetti
Managing Director, Blu Inc Media
former VP Programs, AmCham Shanghai

***

"This book offers a fascinating perspective on the Chinese economy and its culture, from a person with a truly inside view. Mario Cavolo's unique insights, gleaned from a variety of career and personal experiences, are an eye-opener for anyone wanting to understand aspects of China's economy and behavior that are far different than they appear to be on the surface."

Julie H. Hotard, Ph.D.
Psychologist, Seattle, WA

"Unknown trillions are just the tip of the iceberg when it comes to understanding China. Mario's book delivers a deep and true picture like no other China book, it is a must read."

Jacky Cheng
Managing Director, The Scott Partnership, China

***

"Mario Cavolo gives his readers a 'boots on the ground' perspective rarely found in today's literary circles. He not only writes about the real China, he lives and breathes the culture of the Middle Kingdom with each passing day. It is refreshing to read a book about China that delivers a non-biased account of such a diverse and complex society. Cavolo knows this territory better than most."

Gene Kern
President, Emperor Food, China

***

"Mario Cavolo's new book is one to read and ponder. As a sixteen-year resident of China I found his observations and deductions right on target, accurate, and perceptive. It should be required reading for anyone in business and government in the US today, because wealthy Chinese and their children are now outbound. China is not imploding, it is starting to expand outward. In this book Mario describes one of the fuel sources for this movement."

Bill Crampton
CEO, Boombridge, Inc., Guangzhou

***

"You'll never read a more compelling, true and convincing view of the real China. The author handily exposes unknown trillions and masterfully compares and contrasts the driving values and behaviors shaping the dance between the US and China."

Cedric Frignet
Founder & CEO, in-Buzz, Hong Kong

Contents

Acknowledgements .... *xiii*

PART 1

Introduction *1*

The Location of China's Untold Trillions *5*

Consider the Expat Foreigner's View *11*

Behavioral Drivers *13*

The Nine Stories *17*

Defining the "Big Lie" More Precisely *45*

Meet Professor Wang and Credit Suisse *53*

1999: You're Going Where? *57*

Ancient Teachings: Cats, Prozac, and Road Rage *63*

Confucius Says: No Road Rage *65*

Politeness, Etiquette, and Ritual *67*

The Worst Drivers in the World Never Get Angry *75*

Sociology and Confessing to Insanity *79*

Christianity Flourishing and Free in China? *81*

Patriotism: Sacrifice for Country *87*

Get the Flu, Get Robbed *89*

Petty Theft – Getting What You Deserve *91*

Meet a Harvard Trained MD for US$3 .... *93*

Two Extremes Moving Toward the Middle *95*

Lennar Homes NextGen Meets China's "Si Dai Tong Tang" 97
The Cash, the Women, the Baby Boom 101
The Urban Baby Boom Boom Boom 103
Study Abroad 105
In the Driver's Seat 107
Give Me a Call Sometime 109
Blacklisting the World's Largest Retail Economy 111
More on Mortgage Free 117
Saving $200 per Month on a $600 per Month Salary? 121
But Wait—A 50% Savings Rate? 123
Obsessed with Money 125
If You Haven't Tasted a Mango . . . 127
Holding Your Tongue 129
Distortions and Sipping Green Tea 131
Chinese RMB Bank Account: You Mean You Don't Have One Yet? 135
Its Business, Not Politics 137
The Sheer Absurdity that China Has a Real Estate Bubble Ready to Collapse 139
Ninety Percent Home Ownership 141
What Do You Admire Most About Chinese People? 143
China's Tropical Paradise 145
Domestic Vacations 147
Hainan Housing Supply 149
Property Vacancy Rates 151
Development on Par 153
Don't Mistake China's Opening Up as a Warm and Fuzzy Affair 155
Oil's Future Reflected in China's Amazing Green Leap 157
Brief Highlights of China's Rising Wealth 159
The Tax Puzzle 163
Questioning the Wealth Gap 165

A Luxury Car Purchase by the Numbers 167
The US National Export Initiative (NEI) 169
Life Stuck in the Mud? How About $20–$40 per Hour Cash Teaching English? 171
And So . . . 173

Part II
Unrepentant Scrutiny of Reality vs. Myth

Introduction to Part II 179
A "Fly on the Wall" Is Bullish on China (January 2010) 181
A Day in the Life of a Shanghai Consumer (March 2012) 191
Rising Asia Will Soften West's Economic Decline (June 2012) 201
Our Man in China Sees No Global Crash (March 2010) 207
His Rosy Outlook Ignores Reality (March 2011) 215
Slave Labor's Last Gasp (June 2010) 219
Risk of Depression Low Says Our Man in China (July 2010) 223
The Fifteen Trillion Dollar Home Equity Question (January 2010) 233
Can China's Miracle Keep the West Afloat? (August 2010) 241
Asian Money Will Eventually Revive the US (March 2011) 249
Crisis or Circus? (August 2011) 261
Who's to Blame for the Death of the American Middle Class? (October 2012) 265
Behind the Shell Game Lurks a Black Swan (October 2009) 273
Will a Weak Dollar Do Us Any Good? (February 2011) 275

About the Author 279

"I am neither a China cheerleader, nor a China basher; neither pro-China, nor anti-China; neither pro-America, nor anti-America. I am an observer and seeker of reality without judgment to shatter myth vs. reality. We can all see that the dynamics of today's world are both inspiring and frightening. As such, they demand that we see beyond self-interest and without bias."

The Author

Acknowledgements

It was a very special day here in Shanghai. I was the fortunate rainmaker and organizer of a VIP Luncheon event in which we had arranged Asia's legendary former CNN Senior Correspondent and author Mike Chinoy as the guest speaker. Mike was sharing his just-released documentary film, *The Week that Changed the World*, which offers a fascinating, media-centric, behind-the-scenes look at the historical week in US–China relations when then-President Nixon visited China.

It was also true that I was one of the least important people in the room, and that gave me time to reflect on the twelve-year journey that started with the US Consulate in Chengdu inviting me to speak at a series of WTO Conferences across Western China in 1999. I sat listening to opening remarks by Freddie Lee, CEO of the most visible and influential real estate development company in the Asia Pacific region, Shui On Land, who had agreed to be the title sponsor of our event.

Freddie had been handed the CEO reins by Vincent Lo, the man whose name was synonymous with the impressive domain Shui On Land had become in the world of China's commercial real estate market. Mr. Lee's words were charged with the task of offering a message that spoke to the need for more creativity and innovation than ever as we face today's economic, societal, and market challenges while also paying sufficient homage to the events in history that paved the way to China's present status in the world. Next up on the list of guest appearances was Kenneth Jarrett, former US Consul General and Chairman, APCO Greater China, to join Mike for an open panel discussion. I thank these gentlemen and others in similar positions who have taught me so much and enriched my experience of China. It also occurs to me that 40 years onward, neither Nixon nor Mao nor Zhou En Lai could have possibly imagined where their conversation has led us.

As many others would share with respect to their own lives, mine has not been particularly bad or particularly outstanding. As I endlessly strive to identify and fulfill what I believed God's plans and purpose for my life are, the title of the book by well-known Trappist monk and spiritual author Thomas Merton, *No Man Is an Island*, comes to mind. Along the way, our lives are shaped by the impact of those around us. If those experiences were difficult ones filled with regret and darkness, may we learn and grow, in character and in faith.

As those experiences gave us the gift of those people who supported us, contributed to our cause, loved us, perhaps even more than what we had expected, hoped, or deserved, then let's stop and say a heartfelt thank you.

Over the primary two-year period to write this work I engaged with many of my dear friends, business colleagues, and family who offered insights and noticed errors I never would have caught otherwise. My sincerest thanks to each and every one of you. Thanks to my dearest friends for their encouragement and ideas along the way, especially David Turchetti, Daniel Smith, Gene Kerns, and Dr. Allen Brown in Los Angeles. Huge thanks to Cedric Frignet, Ryan McCarthy, Biggie, Morry Morgan, Kerry Kennedy, Nancy Jenster, Peter Harris, Andrea Cristancho, Bill Crampton, ChinaArt Hangzhou, Jason Inch and Andrea, Rick Ackerman and his forum gang, Mike Chinoy, Rory Thomson, Jacky Cheng—my awesome partner in PR, Harry Wong—my awesome partner for over ten years, Jacqueline Simonds with Beagle Bay for starting me off right in North America, and all my clients who appreciate the effort I make to do my best with them.

What is an author but lost without a competent editor? Alex Major from Canada, Richard Trombly based here in China, and Nick MacDonald who is soon heading back to the US after his few years in China; you all did great editing work. Thank you so much.

The editing and design team at Sino Media International, San Francisco / Long River Press quickly impressed me with their professionalism and experience. Even after checking and rechecking dozens of times while working on the manuscript, Chris Robyn sent me back a manuscript for final review with an even higher level of polish and perfection. I am delighted with Sino Media International's decision and support in publishing this ground-breaking work. Thanks to Yang Jing for her diligent efforts to keep the project on track, and let me not skip a special thanks to Tiffany Cha for delivering a striking cover design that was met by an enthusiastic thumbs up by everyone I shared it with for consideration.

Part 1

Introduction

Regarding China, I hope you are asking yourself, is there in fact "A Big Lie"? Is it so meaningful and influential, so unexpected, and so deeply misunderstood that it should be a *Wall Street Journal* headline or on the next *Time* magazine cover? Well, this book explores such an extreme premise: the obvious existence of unknown, uncounted trillions in the domestic Chinese economy, while then moving on to explore that fact and its relationship to other aspects of life, culture, and business in China. If you expect a book that is another inflammatory denunciation of China, or are perhaps looking for me to dispel rumors that China will increasingly dominate the global economy instead of collapsing or remaining content to merely be the manufacturer to the world, I shall say that you will be disappointed.

If you hold the belief that for a multitude of reasons China is going to have some sort of collapse, I strongly doubt you will still hold on to that view even within just the next half hour of reading the first few chapters of this book. And if you don't wish to believe me or other far more qualified experts, a chat with my Chinese mother-in-law will probably get you off the fence.

If however, you are eager to be aware of incredibly important and fascinating knowledge on China, to see things in a new way, to discover fundamental ways of thinking and behavior embedded in China, and to join me in a first-hand account of how China's values and behaviors are generating a sea change that will for all time affect the global economy and its societies, then you have chosen the right book. I should also point out that my intent is not to endorse or praise these trends and developments, but simply for you to be aware of that of which you were previously unaware. I am not a China cheerleader. I am just telling it like it is against a tide of trendy mis- and disinformation that typically focuses on China's myriad problems.

Many such books on controversial topics start with an opinion or a point of view to build their argument and support it as being correct. However, I often notice that authors of such books often employ the easily missed tricks of generalizing, deleting, distorting, mixing truth with half truth, and pointing out the exception to the rule rather than the rule. I assure the reader that throughout this work I have made painstaking effort to avoid such writing. If we were to call this book an argument, then it is an argument that you will soon discover is too easily won. Why is that the case? Because in its approach, you will find my generous use of Sherlock Holmes's favorite method: deduction. I greatly favor deductive reasoning in my approach to understanding many things about life because I feel it leads me to what seems realistically and reasonably true.

The core revelation of this book goes like this: China is awash in trillions of unknown off-the-books cash—somewhere between US$6 and $10 trillion worth—much of it unexpectedly found not in the hands of the top 1% rich, but actually in the hands and lives of the common people. And since most of us are incapable of relating to even one billion dollars, let alone 50 billion or 250 billion dollars, allowing yourself a moment to ponder the force of a few trillion dollars that no one is talking about or officially counting should give enough reason to pause.

By contrast, it is reported in a recent work by University of Wisconsin Professor Edward Feige that the United States' cash economy, commonly called the "shadow economy," now hovers around US$2 trillion, 15% of total US GDP, and since the financial crisis of 2008, it has begun growing significantly. Let me suggest that unemployment statistics spouted by the mainstream media and government don't tell the whole economic story because more and more US citizens are simply and quietly dropping out of the official system. Many of them are not unemployed at all; they are simply doing business directly with one another in cash and barter.

A 2012 article on this phenomenon in the US found at *The Street* notes, "It's not just nannies and waiters and drug dealers being paid under the table. Many friends of mine who once had jobs are now 'freelancers,' or 'small businesspeople,' and most aren't contributing to benefits that used to be a standard part of employment, like retirement and health care. What it means is that the economy is much better than it seems." Another article at *Money News* notes, ..."One example: Explaining why retail sales have outpaced gains in reported income for almost four years, said Bernard Baumohl, chief global economist at the Economic Outlook Group LLC in Princeton, New Jersey.

Amongst China's lower and middle-class citizens, this same phenomenon of living in a cash world is far more prevalent and with a long history. In China's case, the cash economy may be as much as $10 trillion, *equal* to its current official GDP figure—a staggering amount with staggering implications for the rest of the world.

As you read through this body of work, you will find my exploration of additional observable facts of life in China that are interrelated, and you will be more able to decide for yourself how small or large China's cash economy really is, how and why it came to be, and why it is meaningful to be aware of.

This book simply spells out and reveals accuracy and truth as I see it, from my personal, well-researched, and diverse perspective. And I regard these myth-busting truths as being central to the rest of the world's understanding in its need to deal with and respond to the rise of China, which is proving itself to be one of the most influential drivers of this century, for better or worse. That we speak of the rise of Asia led by China is inarguable. That you, the reader, feel its enormity with clarity is my worthy cause.

The Location of China's Untold Trillions

Throughout history we find pivotal moments whereby unknown, undiscovered wealth was hidden in the mountains of Peru, the foothills of frontier California, and most recently, vast reserves of shale gas and oil in the United States.

As never before so explicitly revealed, the world is about to discover one more unexpected frontier, one more remarkable story of untold trillions in an unexpected place. There is however a significant and, for some, hard-to-believe difference as to the source of such wealth, which is the hidden wealth of hundreds of millions of middle class and supposedly lower class Chinese citizens. This wealth quietly exists across the entire income spectrum of the Chinese population, more obviously amongst the wealthy, far less obviously amongst the middle and lower income classes of China who on the surface appear as plain as a generic paper bag.

After reading the well-thought out details of this "Big Lie," I don't know how anyone might still consider refuting it or refuse to believe it. Yet I am troubled—even afraid of a groundbreaking shift in thinking and attitude toward China, which will take hold if that primary assertion is accepted. Agreement that the "Big Lie" is indeed a legitimate reality means acceptance of the reality that within the walls of China exists an additional $6 to $10 trillion dollars in unknown, uncounted, off-the-books cash, much of it held in the hands of the supposed lower- and middle-class citizens. The implications are staggering and easily pointed out by this question: If you suddenly knew that the 20 supposedly poor, hardworking people you were dealing with daily in fact had $100,000 to $500,000 or more in cash in the bank, wouldn't you start responding to them and listening to them in a much different way? I only aim to suggest that you would. You may even feel that they had been duping you by not revealing their true wealth and therefore social status. So let's define the numbers more clearly along the way with specific case examples, at which time I leave it to you, the reader, to conclude how large this unknown mountain of wealth may truly be. Here are three primary assertions I would like to put forth as a framework moving forward:

Assertion 1.

Across China's 26 or so primary first-tier and second-tier cities of urban employed, there are 100 million people whose quiet, practical daily lives are well represented by the nine stories found here. The example stories are about people who are perceived as being in the middle income class. They are the common people, the rule; they are not rare, not the exception. And so, they are a fairly accurate representative sample of the top 100 million income earners within the entire 300–400 million people who make up the rising middle-class population. Let's call them the elite, hardworking entrepreneurs of China.

Note that this assertion assumes we still have 200–300 million urban middle class left whom we assume are earning just enough to get by each year, in the range of RMB 1,500-5,000 per month with perhaps little additional income. They typically have employment in company offices and government offices, restaurants, retailers, etc.

Assertion 2.

Each of these 100 million middle class we are focusing on, which totals less than 10% of the population, have quietly amassed an *average* of $100,000 in off-the-books cash from their efforts and endeavors.

Therefore we calculate 100,000,000 x $100,000 equaling a total of ten trillion dollars. Funny thing is, most of the people whose stories I share with you to demonstrate this idea have far more than that…$500,000 is not a surprise, as surprising as that may seem.

If 1/3 of our elite entrepreneurs have $25,000, 1/3 have $100,000, and 1/3 have $250,000 or more, the total equals $12 trillion. Frankly, that is the proportion and number I most confidently put forth as reasonable and realistic.

Such daily efforts and activities to earn this cash range from simple street-side selling of household items, personal gadgets, and daily clothing to cooking fried eggs and barbecued meats and veggies from a mobile cart on the street for the rush hour employed heading on and off China's subway and bus system. A generous portion of this off-the-books cash is circulating as cash commissions, thank-you referral commissions, which in the West are strictly called kickbacks and which in China are often shared as a traditional Chinese "hongbao," an amount of money handed to you in a pretty red envelope.

Many of these people are earning their income as entrepreneurs, knowing they have no American social security and fancy pension waiting for them in the not-too-distant future. Is it a wonder they learn to somehow save 30% of what little they earn?

"Wai Kuai" in China refers to this extra cash earned in the grey economy, money on the side, which a person earns or receives beyond their known, official, reported salary. The closest we can come to a similar phenomenon in the United States would be the tips of waiters and waitresses and paying cash to the handyman or landscaper, yes? Except in China, unlike America's waiters and waitresses, no such extra cash money is ever officially reported to an organization such as the IRS in the United States for the purpose of collecting income taxes.

If Assertion 1 and Assertion 2 prove as we continue this exploration to be reasonable, then the amount of extra unknown cash in domestic China is at least 10 trillion US dollars above and beyond the officially reported $10 trillion in annual GDP. Seen in that light, you may begin to realize that the officially reported Chinese citizen's average annual income rate of around $3,600 US dollars per year is a number that is laughable at best.

Assertion 3.

Besides having an average of $100,000 cash in the bank, now let's add the matters of ultra-low personal debt and rising mortgage-free home equity wealth. While credit card usage is a new and growing part of

Chinese culture as an import of Western cultures, the vast majority of Chinese citizens still has zero or very low credit card debt balances and by force of daily habitual behavior would never buy anything for which they could not pay cash, not even a car. There will be many more references to this aspect of spending habits in China along the way.

I further hold the rather bullish position that across mainstream China's property market, apartment values are still relatively reasonable (the vast majority of Chinese live in apartments, not individual suburban homes as in the West), prices are too high in some areas but far from a true price bubble, and those prices are unlikely to ever fall below today's values. Considering that 90% of Chinese families own their home, that being the case according to a recent study conducted by Tsinghua University, and that the vast majority of such homeowners have no mortgage, the wealth implications are a staggering addition to the hidden cash wealth we are exploring together.

The remainder of this book is dedicated to helping you the reader to see far more clearly the related underlying values and behaviors in the culture that are driving the Chinese.

So, what, then, is a broader depiction of the "Big Lie" and how will it affect you? We'll start with a few succinct, real-life stories. Together they will lead you to the doorstep of the "Big Lie," to understand it, to reveal why it exists and how it manifests itself throughout China's society.

Each story that follows shares the profile of common, representative individuals who exist in different sectors of Chinese society and who are far more successful and financially stable than anyone knows—except, that is, those directly involved in their affairs. In this description of their stories, you may already begin to realize what the "Big Lie" is and how wise or impious it is in your view.

This phenomenon of a quiet, cash world is certainly cunning in ways and secretive in its character while making corruption much easier, but I would not go so far as to call it devious because all Chinese themselves are very aware of it. So perhaps it would be more fitting to refer to it as the big secret, but you picked up this book or were told about it from a friend because the "Big Lie" is more provocative.

The "Big Lie" shows itself as a characteristic of behavior, even as a Biblical and Confucian principle that is regarded as not only wise and virtuous, but also as clever in Chinese business as well as in society. It is perhaps the key reason that China rose seemingly out of nowhere so suddenly, is now consistently kicking the West's ass and is laughing all the way to the bank.

Oh, sorry, let's not forget that the government still operates the banks; they are not private, for-profit organizations. Banks in China are government held and the Chinese government is the largest holder of foreign reserves at US$3 trillion, including US treasury bonds. While the main theme of this book focuses on the wealth of China's lower and middle income classes, we cannot go without a few observations on China's upper crust. China is a country officially with more than one million millionaires and 63,500 "super rich" according to the 2012 Hurun Wealth Report. The ranks of the multi-millionaires have swelled 49% since 2007 and many trillions of dollars in cash are retained in both the private and government sectors.

Yet you still see images of China as a largely poor and underdeveloped country with an average per capita income of around US$3,000, so how is that possible? The revelation of trillions in off-the-books cash goes far in helping us to understand this great falsehood. The perpetually myopic and misguided media talking heads and supposed China experts like author Gordon Chang somehow keep spinning, spouting, and serving up the ludicrous effluent that "China is about to collapse," which so many Western readers love to naively drink in, like waters from a poison well as they seek to assuage their fears that China is becoming strong. Yes, China is becoming strong, and yes, it is scary in many ways. Yet the country is plagued by challenges well-pointed out, for example, by author Peter Navarro, though I believe his delivery of such information is deeply biased, inflammatory scaremongering, and find far too many generalizations and rule/exceptions violations in his approach.

With a clearer understanding of reality, isn't it true we are then set free from bias? We are then able to interpret its meaning and learn how to find a more advantageous place for ourselves in this developing new global landscape, much of which China is shaping.

I wonder what drives anti-China gurus to continually predict the demise of China by 2005, 2010, now 2012 ad nauseam. With a compilation of seemingly convincing negatives, they have somehow gotten themselves chosen as writers for publications like *Forbes*, yet are still completely, obviously, and demonstrably proven wrong. And every single one of them has never even mentioned to you that China's citizens are sitting on trillions in cash.

To me, that makes such experts who pick and choose the facts to fit their agenda menaces to reality and yet they enjoy the blessing of prestigious media brands. What, then, is their agenda, if not to share and report a fairly accurate, balanced, and realistic picture of China? It is not the purpose of this book to answer that question. I have a healthy disregard for these experts who are perpetual China doomsayers. Why? It is mainly because they are, intentionally or not, deceiving, manipulating, and misguiding you on this critical subject of unprecedented societal and economic impact on the entire world. That really and truly bothers me.

A key intention of explaining the "Big Lie" and related topics is to protect you from feeding into that popular, negative, misleading, media-driven, mainstream thinking on China. In this position, I am not a lone maverick. You will find the views in this book more, though not wholly, in agreement with the positive views of people like investors Jim Rogers, Mark Mobius, author Jason Inch, and investment newsletter guru Robert Hsu. There are a silent host of other businessmen who are here in China quietly and successfully living with keen awareness of what's really going on, and which Chinese don't really want you to know is really going on.

Consider the Expat Foreigner's View

Over 500,000 is a good estimate of the number of foreigners currently living in China. Every one of them I have ever asked about how much money local Chinese people really have wholeheartedly reply with an "Of course." These foreigners are the ones that have made a commitment to live here and become a part of this unfolding epic, recognizing more and more with each passing day how important it is to truly understand the how and why that drives behavior and decisions here.

> "The number of foreigners entering China has been increasing by 10% annually since 2000. Their identities and goals are more diverse than ever, and their activities are wide-ranging and complicated,"
>
> Yang Huanning, vice minister of Public Security

I feel confident suggesting these firsthand views, yet you have every right to question the rigor of my representations from every possible angle. In doing so, push yourself to see past emotional reactions, attachments, and judgments. My work and interests have exposed me to a variety of business areas across the society. Since 1999 I have lived as a full-time resident of China, based in Shanghai. I live here, work here, and have a traditional marriage and family life here with my local Chinese wife, young son, and mother-in-law. I see with my own eyes what is really going on and when I ask those around me if they are seeing the same thing, I get a yes; therefore I deduce it is realistically true and real. I have especially and repeatedly grilled my many Chinese friends and colleagues on these ideas, begging them to tell me if and how I may be mistaken.

I enjoy a diverse lifestyle on both the business and artistic side of life; I occasionally conduct communication skills training for multinational company management and sales people; I have worked in the hotel, media, and events field because of my fun and creative work as an event emcee and jazz pianist. Further related to the media and entertainment industry, I have also had the pleasure of honing my acting and Chinese language skills as an actor in many CCTV China TV mini-series, hosting a culture show for Shanghai Dragon TV, and in an endless number of TV commercials and voiceovers.

Because of this exposure to a variety of experiences across diverse lifestyles and industries, I have more easily than most people here noticed that off-the-books cash is pretty much everywhere, widespread across most every layer and sector of Chinese society and business. It is found in every situation from micro to macro, male to female, friend to foe, child to adult, and from banks to bars to offices and factories, and through the layers of companies ranging from small- to medium-sized enterprises (SME) to huge multinational companies of every name brand you can think of.

Though it must be said that many recognized international brand name companies are drawing a strict, hard line against China's world of cash kickbacks, and while it is an uphill battle, the phenomenon is in decline in those business circles. Education organizations such as CEIBS MBA school and many other foreign MBA programs and Chinese universities are drivers of compliance with international law and transparency. One of the respected leaders of CEIBS shared with me their thought that they could not endorse this book in any public way because even though they realize I am just reporting such practices, it could be perceived that the book is endorsing such practices. I then thought it would be a perfect idea to have them write and include their view of such ethical and compliance issues in the book, but they declined to do so.

Behavioral Drivers

You have by now realized I am not by any means calling Chinese liars regarding their off-the-books cash any more than I would stereotypically call New Yorkers rude, Germans stoic, or French snooty. Such pronouncements are overreaching, one-sided stereotypes. These are silly, thin veneers. It is not about overtly lying, it is a default behavior and choice in dealing with others, whether with each other as Chinese, or with foreigners. The "Big Lie" of unknown, off-the-books trillions is a deeply embedded mindset in the fabric of Chinese society, a "way of thinking," driven by underlying personal and societal values. This mentality is a method for dealing with one another in this massive population of 1.3 billion, for dealing with foreigners here and with the outside world.

You may start to resist my thesis as a form of closed mindedness or prejudice. However, those of us who are long-term foreigners living here in China realize that Chinese people "think" differently than we do and it is a most singular factor we remain ever mindful of. In addition, when professional, English-speaking, white-collar Chinese citizens read this book, they have the same unanimous reaction as the experienced foreigners who live here: "We know this."

There is a deep, ingrained Asian mindset that developed along different lines than our Western culture. There is no value judgment being made, but one would be foolish to live here for long or do business here and not recognize this. It is simply a different and equally valid cultural reality and my dear Chinese friends regard it as obvious and normal and wise.

While a shadow cash economy makes it easier for corruption to flourish, the "Big Lie" of cash trillions does not lead us to a question of good or evil with respect to individual Chinese people or the Chinese government. Across the entire world, the "black market" economy traditionally refers to off-the-books cash earned by illegal activities such as gun running and drug dealing while the grey shadow economy refers to off-the-books cash earned in legitimate, acceptable pursuits.

In China, the "Big Lie" is an obvious known hidden right in front of everyone. Honest, genuine people along with cheaters and scam artists know no country borders. Whether we are dealing with ethical, honest, and genuine folks or selfish cheaters with no scruples who wish only to separate us from our money is a separate matter from the existence of a widespread, off-the-books, grey shadow economy. To try to overcome it, to ignore it, or to force your way in to somehow defeat it would be like taking a shield and spear to fight the flow of the mighty Yangtze River that flows by Shanghai into the China Sea. But you can learn to recognize it, understand it, and take it for what it is—an indelible and essential element of Chinese society.

Let's examine more shades of grey. In America, people typically accuse issuers of statistics of making them look better than they really are. We might suggest as an example that the government issues official inflation statistics that are low compared to the real inflation that the average consumer feels. Wall Street is often accused of employing whatever tricks it can, such as "mark to market," to make the numbers look better to concerned investors. What might be another example? How about unemployment statistics? Who would ever accuse the United States government of intentionally releasing unemployment statistics that were worse than they really are? Instead in the West, it has become commonplace for most any American to immediately think to themselves, "Oh, no, real unemployment is higher than that!" True or not, please remember my purpose here is to identify a common default "mindset" in the way people think and fulfill "expected behavior" in a particular society.

How much do you read about core, value-driven human behavior in the Western media articles and books on China? Very little. Many of these journalists and more than a few scholars honored as "experts" we listen to have never set foot beyond the cities of modern, international Shanghai, manufacturing bases in Guangdong, and just a stone's throw from the Hong Kong border or the corridors of political power in Beijing. As these experts are lead around the typical destinations for foreigners, do they honestly think they can pierce this silken curtain and see what lies beneath, or, like an iceberg, are they looking only at the tip?

The Nine Stories

To live here as a foreigner, one must become aware of what both hands are doing or find oneself continually confused, disappointed, and confounded. So now let me share with you a few real-world stories of life in "Zhong Guo," which translates as the "Middle Kingdom" between Heaven and Earth, as China so humbly regards itself.

These nine stories introduce you to representative Chinese middle-class people who are simply far better off, far more entrepreneurial, and far more successful in their life than we might imagine. As these people lead a humble and low-key existence, I have done them the service of protecting their privacy, name, and identity, altering minor details to obscure location and background, rather than expose bare their privacy. The pertinent details of each story are genuine and accurate.

Many of us consider the old biblical reference in Matthew's gospel referring to the left hand not knowing what the right hand is doing. I would say that the Chinese have this value as a part of their moral and ethical code; they never let the left hand see what the right hand is doing, as a matter of self-preservation and self-protection—for good or bad purposes and ends I leave you to judge.

At the end of the stories you are about to read, I will more broadly define the "Big Lie." May I suggest you don't jump ahead and instead allow yourself to first enjoy stepping into their lives, into the shoes of another person's world.

Story I: Young Mr. Li's Investment Portfolio

Chengdu, China, 1999

I knew something wasn't right. My good buddy Mr. Li was obviously fraught with anxiety.

It was winter 1999 and Chengdu was the first city in China I had come to live. I was enjoying another set of spicy, incredibly tasty Sichuan dishes over lunch with my friend Mr. Li, who had become a close friend over many months since I had settled down there.

He was a fine, ambitious, young man in his mid 20s. Still single and stick-thin with a hawkish beak for a nose, Mr. Li lived with his parents who had a comfortable apartment on the Sichuan University campus where they were teachers for many years on salaries around RMB 2,000 per month. As is also common in such situations, the university also provided the family with modest housing at little or no cost. I may mention I know of another such school teacher who was 20 years earlier able to buy a common yet very nice 85-square-meter, two-bedroom apartment for around RMB 50,000, or US$6,000 (currency adjusted). All such comfortable family apartments across China's second-tier cities today are valued at ten times that amount—RMB 500,000, or US$82,000 (currency adjusted). But let me not digress from the story of our Mr. Li's investment portfolio.

I knew that as the principal of an English school associated with Sichuan University, he was earning RMB 2,400 per month, still substantially higher than most local Chinese second-tier city wages, which are closer to RMB 1,000 per month.

At that time RMB 2,400 was equal to US$300 and is now worth US$400. By the way, when we use the word "salary" in China, it typically means your take-home pay rather than gross pay before deductions.

Finally, my friend revealed the source of his anguish. His stock portfolio for 1999 was down—the market was particularly treacherous that year! He later told me the balance:

US$60,000 / RMB 360,000.

Thankfully, I was sitting down at the time. Did such an unexpectedly high sum of cash come from his well-off parents? Couldn't be so, I mused and pondered, as they were simple schoolteachers on salaries even lower than his.

In Mr. Li's case, I can say that the accumulation took place slowly over a few years through a combination of very low monthly budget expenses, diligent, disciplined savings of over 30% of salary each month, and Mr. Li's variety of efforts as a young entrepreneur to make some extra money on the side, which he diligently set aside.

Story II: Standing in Line at the Bank

Sanya, Hainan Island, 2004

I was standing in the lobby when I happened to glance in his direction and had barely noticed it.

Sanya is a local coastal city, an oasis of classic, tropical, beachfront resorts at the southern-most point on China's tropical Hainan Island, also one of its provinces. This is rightly China's most popular and most well-developed resort destination and the place where my wife and I lived starting in 2007, for the first three years of our marriage before then moving back to Shanghai in 2010. You might have pictures in your mind of cold, snowy Beijing winters and humid, polluted mega-cities in the south such as Guangzhou, so is it strange to envision a tropical paradise in China?

In fact, Sanya is located quite farther south toward the equator than one might think. On a map, you will find it is 300 km due east of Hanoi, Vietnam, complete with classic tropical weather and beaches surrounding a lush, mountainous rainforest island. As with many worthy tropical escapes across the world, it is easy to forget where you are—whether it is the sun-blazed splendor of the Caribbean, Mexico, the Mediterranean, or Southeast Asia.

On Hainan Island, just like on those above-mentioned tropical islands, soon after leaving the modern five-star hotels, you find yourself immersed in a very rough and rustic street culture of dingy shops and street food vendors delivering bargain-priced meals and cheap wares to the host of locals that service the tourist trade and pander to their every need. You will find a similar dark underbelly of rough streets and rustic dwellings beyond the gates of North America's tropical paradises as well. But there is one huge, unexpected difference.

It was while standing in the lobby of the Jiefang Lu branch of the Bank of China in downtown Sanya when I glanced and noticed it.

The old, tattered, nylon bag.

Its owner was a local Hainanese man standing in one of the other teller queues; a thoroughly unimpressive, shoddy-looking character, sun-baked skin revealing the lines of age, keeping to himself as anyone might do standing in line at the bank, all the subtleties of which my mind whirled together and certainly contributed to why I noticed not his bag, but its unexpected bulk.

Typical of the locals, this particular gentleman was probably a local craftsman or fisherman, with no more than ten years of rudimentary countryside, elementary schooling, speaking only the local dialect, not the country's common Mandarin, and it was reasonable to construe that he possessed poor reading skills at best.

He might have been a small business owner. In China and other third-world countries, that may mean having no more than an old, filthy, three-square-meter shop space along the street where he and his family live on old chairs and cots in a single room behind the shop's rear wall or perched in a crudely built loft of wooden planks above it. Let's complete the picture by imagining a strung rope hanging across the back side of the store on which the family's laundry hangs idly to dry, noting that even most rich people in China still don't use electric clothes dryers; the front street-side corner of the space reveals a single coal-fired wok pot for cooking, perhaps instead a single-burner propane stove top.

If I happened to see him along the street at sunset along with other locals gathering at the outdoor restaurants for dinner, he might sit at one of the many raggedy, local restaurants that line the pavement serving delicious if greasy and unbelievably cheap food with $0.50 bottles of northern China's Snow or local brand Hainan beer.

Stalking him further through the city might take us back to his own apartment, with our trail leading to an equally dingy, dirty apartment building. There is also a high likelihood that the four generations of his family all live there together, another important aspect of understanding China that we will take a closer look at.

The old tattered bag was closely held to his body, yet he found himself habitually opening and checking it a few times as he passed the time. Accounting for its bulk, it was loaded with cash; several six inch stacks of RMB 100 notes, each neatly wrapped individual bundle valued at RMB 10,000 (US$1500), four or five stacks filling the space, totaling perhaps US$40,000 to $50,000.

Such an affront to my senses—a dazzling, dizzying disparity between the plain, simple truth and my judgmental expectations and assumptions of reality.

This moment was the second time since learning of Mr. Li's woeful investment portfolio that the "Big Lie" was staring me in the face so palpably, so alive. In stereotypical terms, this guy looked like a real lowlife. How much of an exception or rule did this man represent? I look back and realize this was the time in my life in which began a shift in my own mindset, now noticing much more that which we don't usually notice, more consistently probing and deducing the answer to the questions, "What's really going on here? These people seem to have a lot more money than meets the eye; why and what else does that tell me about this place?"

Yet to a few hundred million Chinese all across the country doing what they do each day, my inquiring mind was pondering a given, something not even worth noticing. Why would you notice something so common, right?

Just the way they like it.

Story III: Mrs. Yan the Frumpy Breakfast Lady

Shanghai, March 2011

Mrs. Yan is a frumpy, old, retired lady; a street vendor selling $0.75 fried egg wraps from her rusty, coal-fired, portable wheeled cart for breakfast in our neighborhood. In the cold, wet winters, with its coal-fired metal barrel below, such crude equipment quickly dismissed as unspeakable junk elsewhere works dual wonders as both an income-generating café on wheels and a toasty warm heater.

A note penned to Mrs. Yan might read like this:

"Dear Mrs. Yan,

Do you recall that nice, local foreigner guy with the pregnant wife from northern China who came around to your street cart for one of your tasty egg wrap things this morning for breakfast? Yes, right, that tall, Italian-looking guy with the wife from Dongbei (Northeast China) who talks more than most, that's the one. Did you know that he is writing about little ol' you in his book, his market analysis and commentary on China, on the Sino-American, socio-political, and economic landscape across international media and investment advisory websites reaching across the entire planet feverishly discussing the critical global issues and trends impacting our increasingly, instantaneously, interconnected world? Hmm, didn't think so. And you don't understand why he would do that? That's not a surprise either, so let's find out why, dear Mrs. Yan, you're the talk of the town from where I'm sitting."

Let's take the economic and societal issues of the day across the globe down to earth, let's make it real, and make it human, starting with eggs. Specifically the egg wraps Mrs. Yan makes from her street cart every morning seven days a week from 6 to 9 a.m. at subway line #2, Century Park, on the Pudong side of the river in the heart of Shanghai. By this closer look at reality, we can understand with amazing clarity, for example, how and why it is that Chinese millionaires and almost-millionaires are heading to America with lots of cash in hand to buy and invest, a phenomenon I believe will have a significant impact on America's societal and economic future.

We need to understand our world, each and every one of us who has concern for what is happening across the social and economic landscape, to understand the most important force in the world today: Asia rising meets dollar falling. Some might say that sounds a bit like a bad date. In the interest of valuable insights and enjoying a good read that will probably make you hungry for one of the 200-plus tasty fried egg wraps Mrs. Yan churns out each morning, here's the account of what was otherwise a typical morning in the neighborhood, the morning I met Mrs. Yan.

As I was rolling still half asleep out of bed this morning, my predictably picky, pregnant wife asked me to go out and get her one of those local egg wrapped in a crepe kind of things she likes from her favorite street vendor, Mrs. Yan. This is one of the few foods my wife enjoys eating these days with her taste and scent buds so out of whack, such things are not a myth for pregnant women. We live just a one-minute stroll to the nearby subway line in a lovely, older local neighborhood on the south side of Century Park here in Pudong. It is a perfect urban Shanghai location. One minute's walk to the city's largest park is perfect for my running routine. Less than five minutes away is the Maglev high-speed line, whisking us at 400 km per hour to Pudong International airport in 12 minutes. Driving our car, we're over the Nanpu Bridge and into the famed Puxi side of town in less than 15 minutes. Near perfect transportation convenience available from our quiet, local, tree-lined neighborhood here in Shanghai, the most happening city in the world as proclaimed by a *Time* magazine cover a couple of years back. And that was before the World Expo 2010, which did far more for China's international reputation than teach Disney a thing or two about daily attendance records.

As the locals stream along the streets down to the subway, street vendors are out hustling with their portable breakfast carts—think New York hot dog stands, but far older and dirtier, with big, rusty, crooked wheels. From our Western point of view, Mrs. Yan looks to you and me as a hard-working street person; frumpy, retired, unkempt, worn down, little education. She is all of the above, ordinary amongst the common.

Mrs. Yan kicks butt on the streets of Shanghai and she's been doing it every day for the past 15 years. Mrs. Yan serves up 200 of her one-minute-fast, fresh, fried egg wrap things from her coal fired flat iron stove top on wheels every morning at RMB 4 each—that's about US$0.75 each. She starts by spooning a ladle of pancake batter on the griddle top, heated from below by coals. Within a minute, she cracks and spreads on a fresh egg, some seasoning, gives it a final flip and fold, and off you go. Her food cost, my wife and I calculated, is less than $0.25. Mrs. Yan then repeats this feat in the late afternoon, selling instead fried meat skewers, hot dogs, breads. A little calculating tells us that our dear, frumpy Mrs. Yan quietly earns around $120 per day seven days per week. Add it up to RMB 18,000/ US$3,000 per month. She is far richer than most, living in her modest 70-square-meter apartment with her husband who probably had a salaried job as an engineer at $300 per month for the past 20 years.

With typical local monthly living expenses around $600 or less, that means Mr. & Mrs. Yan have socked away close to $180,000 every five years for the past fifteen years totaling $540,000 not including interest. Better than a great bank heist movie script, that's Mrs. Yan's cool half million in cold, hard, tax-free cash.

Mrs. Yan hides her cart in the apartment garden behind the gate at 9 a.m. That's when the police come on duty and might otherwise come and take her stuff because she is in fact, as many, an unlicensed street vendor. In some places the police are more vigilant about preventing unlicensed businesses and street vendors, for the simple fact that they didn't obtain the proper street vendor license and of course, don't pay any taxes on their income That is reasonable, if the tax rates are reasonable, which they are. But in cities of 10–15 million people, this way of merchant street life thrives on, proper license or not.

Here is where I perpetually struggle, feel the fear of failure in my cause to impress you with the implication of undressed reality. Take the above scene and wash, rinse, repeat for millions of people every day across China where the merchant survival lifestyle is the root of the lower/middle class and invisible cash is king to the tune of untold trillions of dollars starting with Mrs. Yan's cool half a million.

Poor street people with half a million dollars cash. At least when you see them on the street, that's what you assume; that they are poor people. Now you recognize they are simple people, but not unfortunate, poor people.

Merchants

Authentically poor people are people who don't have a reasonable means available to them to be productive. My paternal grandfather was a barber while my maternal grandfather was first a delivery truck driver, a fish market owner, then a soda fountain stationery store owner where we grew up around Yonkers, New York. They were merchants.

The local, retail-merchant-style living is what American society moved away from and has contributed greatly to the decline of the middle class, which has become more and more dependent on the plans of large corporations and government than ever. Manufacturing went away too, plus the blatant banking industry shenanigans that make us all want to vomit. Throw in a generous measure of really bad self-serving governance for a recipe that has pummeled the lifestyle of the lower and middle classes.

So, now what? Big trouble for America's lower and middle classes, not nearly so for China's poor street people or farmers. China's "poor" farmer's have a stone or brick building to live in with coal heat in the wintertime and all the food they want 24/7. I'd be comfortable suggesting it's more like camping than being poor. Or would you rather live in a downtown tenement building under the unspoken, fear-riddled rule of weapon-wielding, drug-peddling gangs? In my book, poor is having to walk through a metal detector at school or at a nightclub when all you want to do is go out with your date and enjoy a night of drinking and dancing. Yet, an American might say that poor is not being able to freely say that the leader of your country is an incompetent jerk. Who's really poor? Who's really free? Maybe that's the big lie.

Even noted as recently as Double Line Funds founder Jeff Gundlach's 2012 presentation on the economy, "To Catch A Thief," US wages have been declining while corporate profits have been rising to record highs. How's that for unfair in the land of the free? I hope it annoys you and that collectively, such trends shift in America's future.

Yet, embedded in that big trouble is the polar energy called opportunity, which will come via Mrs. Yan's cool half a million cash flowing into America; as she comes to tour, to shop, to enjoy the freshness of a new destination, to send her child to a US university, and to buy up the bargain real estate. The trend is already in full force with typical Chinese tour groups spending and investing far more than any other foreign visitors to American shores, because she just wants to give herself and her children options—not perfect options, but reasonable options and choices. As we then raise the scale of this trend to the new, far richer Chinese people and companies who are also looking to spread their wealth, give themselves options, and expand their investment opportunities across the globe, we suddenly see more clearly how the new world works and what the future will look like.

So, then, some have asked, why would they invest in America? For two reasons, both strong and intertwined; because they are pragmatic opportunists who love a bargain, and because they still see all the advantages and great things about America through a romantic eye, even with the current issues America faces. They keenly have their eye on America—trust me, believe me, they do. They see China's problems, all the rottenness of China as clearly as many see the rottenness of America.

Both countries, far from perfect yet perfect complements to each other's differences. And so they have a very high level of interest to diversity, to protect themselves via such diversification as establish life and business and investment across the Pacific in America. Be thankful for the economic power that the rise of Asia led by China will bring to America's shores in the coming years, in her time of need, in her need to recover from an unprecedented—and yes, shameful—debt hangover. The next five years will be rough but will gradually also build the foundational trends over the next five years leading to rebuilding, restructuring, and new opportunities that will emerge.

This incoming wave to America also applies at the academic level. See the "Study Abroad" chapter for further details. Who are the high-scoring students in college? The Chinese, the Asians. Where do they want to study more than anywhere else? America. Let me tell you bluntly: Even as America has her problems as a country, to any Chinese, an American passport or green card is still regarded as a holy grail of freedom. The word for America in Chinese is "Mei Guo," which means beautiful country, and the nouveau riche Chinese want

America. Rightly so, while I will not hesitate to point out America's many serious problems, I also quickly note that in many ways America is a spectacular place both geographically and with respect to its many beautiful, genuine people.

Let's not forget this story begins with Mrs. Yan churning out $0.75 egg wraps, a little, one-woman, frumpy food factory, day in and day out, keeping her mouth shut, quietly doing her thing, appearing and disappearing like a mystical ninja ghost warrior. Nonsense, she's just doing her best to survive and help her children have a better future.

We shall not forget that our Mrs. Yan is doing business illegally without a license, but at least she is not selling illegal goods. Along the same streets we find vendors selling bootleg DVD's, CD's, and books at $1.50 each. They can also be viewed as commonplace, hard-working entrepreneurs also doing what they must, except those products cross the line into pirate goods, not tasty egg wraps to fill a hungry belly.

China's street vendors are omnipresent. They shape and weave the fabric of the culture here, offering everything from fresh fruit to barbecue, bootleg DVD's, clothes and shoe shines. For now, when you think of all the cash that more and more Chinese show up with to spend and invest on America's shores, often in pursuit of America's EB-5 investment visas residence program, think of Mrs. Yan, her street fresh, fried egg wraps, her cool, quiet half a million, and all that such a local saga implies for the rest of the world.

Story IV: Ms. Wang, Small Business Owner in Corporate Training

Shanghai

Ms. Wang, single, 24 years old in 2004 when she registered her own small company to provide corporate training services to the many Chinese and multinational companies experiencing rapid growth and so easily falling behind in the quality of leadership, management, and communication skills needed to compete and run a successfully company. It is one thing to have 15 or 40 employees. When one year later you have 250 to 500, management now faces a new and big problem. Typically, the high potential leaders emerge, personality- and talent-wise, from within the organization but are still sorely lacking in the skills to manage and deal with people effectively.

There is, in fact, little in the way of someone such as our Ms. Wang from seeing the opportunity, registering a company, renting a small startup office, finding a handful of qualified corporate trainers to deliver programs, and then simply contacting the HR Directors of the many companies who need such training. Such corporate training is typically billed out at US$1,500-$2,500 per day for a workshop while the local training company pays out a percentage of the contract to the trainer who conducts the workshop, leaving a tidy profit after minimal expenses.

This is the perfect illustration of a simple, small business startup in the right place at the right time to deliver a need in a still rapidly growing marketplace. Rapidly growing large domestic and multinational companies face a shortage of employees with good management, technical, organizational, and people skills.

It also helps when several of your best friends from school now work in the HR/admin departments of your target companies and it further helps that Ms. Wang will, as is customary, kickback about 10 to 15% of the contract back to those HR employees, her friends.

There are now well over 300 corporate training companies in Shanghai; a nonsensical, brutally competitive number that belies typical business model profitability and viability, except when you understand how well the "Big Lie" perfectly fits in. Ms. Wang quietly goes about her business with a small handful of perhaps two to five key clients. She lives an unassuming life, works a lot, and the additional post-invoice cash she shares back with her alumni friends probably totals from $10,000 to $30,000 cash per year beyond their own salary and compensation package. Let's take this picture ten years out into the future and now we easily see how professional employees pay cash for everything they buy, whether it be a new $30,000 car, a new $300,000 apartment, or their children's college education in Europe.

Speaking of $300,000, what real estate property can $300,000 actually buy in today's China?

One 100-square-meter, $300,000 apartment in a very nice area of a first-tier city such as Shanghai, Beijing, Shenzhen, Guangzhou is very expensive, calculated at RMB 30,000 per square meter = US$500 per square foot. Exceptional super-prime locations such as Lu Jia Zui in Shanghai go for double that rate and more, and are often the locations cited in China real estate bubble stories. However, such locations and prices are the exception, not the rule, of the mainstream marketplace.

Three nice 100- to 125-square-meter, $100,000 apartments in a secondary area, such as outside of Shanghai, or located in a growing second-tier city such as Shenyang or Chengdu. , and even including a tropical beachfront condo in Sanya, Hainan Island, or perhaps overseas in Thailand or Malaysia. Average prices at RMB 8,000–10,000 square meter = US$160 square meter. Today, many of China's second- and third-tier cities also offer reasonable apartments in the lower RMB 4,000-8,000 range. Yesterday's Chinese apartments found in the range of RMB 1,000–3,000 per square meter are pretty much gone forever, following similarly in the footsteps of the US real estate market from the '50s to the '90s except with such expansion and price appreciation happening over a single decade, a much shorter period of time in comparison.

With a 30% mortgage down payment requirement, $300,000 cash down lets you buy a $750,000 private 300-to 400-square-meter, three-story villa with a fifteen year $450,000 mortgage on which your payment will be around US$3,000 a month.

I recall Ms. Wang bought herself a new $150,000 apartment in a prime Shanghai location in 2007, which as luck and timing goes in China today, is now worth four times that. She's done and she's barely 30. I seriously doubt the value of such prime location Shanghai apartments will go down any more than I believe that the value of a prime location apartment in Manhattan, London, San Francisco, Paris, or Tokyo will also go down from current high-price levels even after the US real estate crash. Please think about this observation very clearly for a moment: the higher real estate prices today in prime Chinese cities are in line with and similar to prices of real estate in prime international cities all across the world.

And don't get tired of hearing it: Ms. Wang paid cash for her apartment; she has no mortgage. Not bad for someone in her mid-20s, who can be regarded as virtually common, white collar middle class; perhaps we can call her quietly invisible, just doing her thing.

Story V: Those Lazy Spaniards?

There are a lot of retired people hanging around the local apartment neighborhoods in China on low pensions with equally low expenses. Their life is simple. They play cards, the men smoke cigarettes, they chat away the day, they meet at the local park or square and dance/exercise to Chinese songs blaring on an old boom box. Many gather with their grandchildren while mom and dad are off to work all day long. They are remarkable at their ability to be content with what they have and where they are in life.

Some of them on the other hand, are the loud ones, such as my friend Mr. Liu, possessing far more colorful, outspoken personalities than the average.

One day, as I was hanging around for a few minutes with the locals in our neighborhood, we got to talking about a variety of affairs; things like the economy, rising cost of living, unemployment across the world, etc.

I spoke up about the current affairs in Europe as I stated, "Europe is in very bad shape these days. In Spain, unemployment is up to 25%!"

Mr. Liu's unapologetic, passionate, dismissive reply was one word:

"Lan!"

with the accompanying boisterous wave of his arm through the air that one might expect.

"Lan" in Mandarin means "lazy."

In less than two seconds, Mr. Liu set things straight for each and every one of us. In his view, much of which can quite easily be agreed with,

25% unemployment amongst the poor miserable citizens of Spain is unadulterated nonsense. In his view, at least half of those 25% of people who are unemployed, whether in Spain or any other country, are lazy excuse makers, vexed by their own stubborn pride, their refusal to accept reality, to create work for themselves or to take a job they don't want at pride-swallowing lower pay.

Mr. Liu went on to point out the obvious, and when I say obvious, I do mean in your face everywhere you look. He just started pointing in every direction around our local neighborhood at all the people on the street who are there day and night selling whatever goods or service they can to make a living; the fruit and food vendors, the shoe shine folks, the motorcycle taxis, the folks unraveling their blankets to sell jewelry, baby socks, kitchen accessories, you name it. Sure, we do realize half of them do not have any proper business license from the government to do so and so the police come around occasionally to chase them away, to make them move, ticketing them, harassing them, annoying them, making it difficult for some of them to earn enough of a living just to survive.

Now imagine with me a similar story of reality, struggle, and success during the time of my childhood: my mother at home raising myself and two brothers on Cowles Avenue in Yonkers, New York. Around the corner, many years after a post-military career as a barber with his father Frank, and now my father owning and running Mario's Stationery store seven days a week, my mother going down to help when she possibly could arrange it.

Later on, my dad sold the stationery store for a modest sum in his effort to build a more secure future and I recall well that he held four jobs at once. While struggling to become a successful salesman of life insurance, he also sold vending machines in the tri-state area, sold the *Encyclopedia Britannica* door to door, and on weekends, was a wedding photographer for a local wedding studio. On top of all that, he spent several years going part time to Columbia University to educate himself.

So with those memories of my own father in mind, don't mind me for agreeing with Mr. Liu's view on the real story behind government and media-driven public statistics like Spain's 25% unemployment. Yet, let me expressly disallow any misunderstanding on this point; whether it be Spain or any other country, many people truly are victims of circumstance brought on by the poor choices and self-serving greed and corruption of people in charge of both companies and governments worldwide. Surely there is much truth in that view and it is the constant battle for a better life, against unfairness that many humans across the world face on a daily basis. That said, there comes in every individual human being's life the day to accept unfortunate reality, to accept change, to squarely see one's own choices each step of the way, and do what one must in the present moment.

Which just might mean getting four jobs like my dad had done.

Next we put our attention on the local police in China, who also know our neighbor Mrs. Yan from Story III. They know exactly who our quietly rich street merchant Mrs. Yan is and what she is doing each day. They know that many of the street merchants are, in fact, raking in plenty of cash, living quiet, acting poor, yet illegally accumulating their $1,000 or $2,000 or more per month, cash, without paying any taxes and with very low monthly expenses. So, can we say the police are wrong in their effort to enforce the law when they do so? Or, as the police themselves are also on low state salaries, would it surprise us if an officer might look the other way in return for a share, thus participating themselves in the street's cash economy? While cash business amongst private citizens is particularly difficult to track, such activities by higher level government officials and public sector employees are being more and more scrutinized by the Chinese government. The higher your position, the higher your profile and responsibility to fiscal stewardship, the more likely you are to get caught. On the heels of many other such government officials, the ex-mayor of Chengdu and head of China's Ministry of Railways are the next on the chopping block now being investigated and convicted for corruption, with death not being an unlikely sentence.

Likewise, go ahead and try to be a street entrepreneur in the United States to make some extra money to support your family and pay your bills and see what happens. I remember reading a headline a few years ago at Yahoo News. Here, I am paraphrasing:

Chinese government raids and closes down over 50 Internet bars in Beijing. I read four paragraphs of obligatory "cracking down on censorship, no freedom of speech," blah, blah, blah.

While just a bit wiser than the average reader on such pointless China-bashing narratives, I noticed one brief yet brilliantly clarifying sentence buried in the article text:

"...for operating illegally without a business license."

Oh, my, that certainly clarifies what is really going on, don't you think?

Try opening any storefront business in the United States without a business license. You can't even get past "go." Typically, there are multiple inspections from various local and state and federal government, utility and industry regulation officers along the way before you would even be granted permission to open the door. I can tell you from personal experience that's the way it is in the US restaurant business as I recall an electrical inspector at our family's Peter Piper Pizza restaurant kitchen in Scottsdale insisting I relocate an electric socket two inches further up the wall before I dare to open the front door for business. Such regulatory infrastructure is and has been clearly in place for many decades while also having become even stricter and more expensive to comply with in the United States. We can easily state that some of such regulatory oversight is important and valuable in its service to the community at large and we are mostly glad and fortunate it exists to create a safer, more consistent experience in our daily lives. In contrast, food safety and contamination is a huge, ongoing problem in China precisely because it is so difficult to enforce laws in such a massively populated and fast-growing country. Such oversight is less widespread, there are five times more people running around per square kilometer. Yet, I remind you we are not here to argue those pros and cons, only to state and see reality as it is, to know where the cash is. And so today, compared to the United States, it is still far easier in China to get away with quietly opening many types of business without going through the legal required procedures along the way before you can be up and running, raking in the cash, yet leaving the door open to more violations of safety and ethics by China's "hei xin ren," which in English translates as the people with black hearts.

Story VI: Irrational Fear of the Chinese Hospital System

While living in Newport Beach, California, in the early 2000s, I once attended a seminar featuring the legendary American motivational speaker Jim Rohn. As many such experts on stage, Jim could stand in front of an audience with no notes for days and talk and talk and talk. I recall a colleague of mine asking him during a break, "Jim, it is amazing to watch you; how can you stand in front of us for so many hours and talk without any notes and never miss a beat?"

Jim replied, "It's easy! Just do it a couple thousand times!"

And so with kudos to Mr. Rohn's skill as a master due to repetition, I turn our attention to the birth of babies in China and wonder:

"Hey, these maternity department and maternity hospital doctors and nurses deliver thousands of babies every month and have been doing so for 20 years in a country of 1.3 billion people, so just maybe they know what they're doing."

It is disquietingly common to hear the fear-ridden remarks of corporate expats coddled by their really expensive company-paid health insurance, that they would *only* go to their insurance-covered international hospital and to say they would *never* step foot in a *Chinese* hospital. Hearing horror stories of poor medical care in China and paying homage to the broad, sweeping, ultra-safe "better safe than sorry" approach, it is as if it would never occur to them that a Chinese hospital might actually be capable of delivering high quality healthcare and has competent doctors. I could suggest they more enjoy justifying the existence of their sweet benefit package rather than wondering if it is really necessary in the first place. I can tell you from thirteen years of personal experience placing myself in the care of Chinese hospitals for a variety of my own health issues that I will confidently continue placing myself and my family in the care of those same hospitals and doctors in the years to come. If the past thirteen years' experiences were not satisfactory enough, I would certainly not.

More specifically with regard to the experience of pregnancy and birth, I now present to you a composite picture of the experience of eight couples including my wife and myself, who all chose to have their pregnancy/birth services at a typical local Chinese city hospital; either Di Yi Fu Ying Maternity Hospital, which in English reads, First Maternity Hospital, or Ping An Hospital, which in English is the International Peace Hospital. Every couple had a completely satisfying experience from the onset of their pregnancy through the ongoing checkups and birth without a complaint. The average bill without health insurance came to US$1,500 or about RMB 10,000, with the low being closer to $1,000 and the higher range reaching a total close to $3,000. Most of the couples I refer to were expat couples, a foreign man with a Chinese wife, while two couples in our group were typical, local Chinese couples who have been friends of ours for many years.

During the health care process we all experienced from pregnancy to the post-birth period, every few weeks the woman goes for a routine checkup that includes an ultrasound every three months. Mothers are well instructed on various self-care interests, what to eat and not eat, placed on pre-natal multi-vitamins, and are encouraged to be active but careful and not too active. Alcohol, caffeine, sugar substitutes, and all such suspect substances are to be completely avoided. Dads-to-be are involved every step of the way, able to stay with mom-to-be during the checkup including the ultrasound, enjoying taking photos and watching the technicians go through their process of measuring and recording the size and various parts of the unborn baby and other relevant observations.

It is against the law in China for the doctors or nurses to tell you the gender of the baby as to discourage any idea to abort a female, a choice that we understand comes from the archaic country farm idea that a boy is stronger to work the land or business and support the family. Fortunately, such controversial choices as a gender abortion are declining in Chinese society, and did you know that the gender abortion problem is far worse in India, with over 3,000 local ultrasound clinics scattered across the country?

During one of the wives' third trimester, the doctor raised a minor concern and recommendation as follows:

"You are a small woman (I do mean small! Many Chinese men and women are 90 lbs. soaking wet) and it is no surprise that your baby is also on the small side, a bit below the lower side of the standard weight range we look for. Therefore, we would like you to stay in the hospital for a week and give you the following regimen":

You will eat a steady, high-protein diet of meats, fish, and vegetables.

By daily IV drip, we will give you additional amino acids and vitamins.

We will administer one course of betamethasone corticosteroid treatment to boost the baby's lung development.

By doing this, you will avoid the hustle and bustle of your daily life, which is probably interfering with keeping you relaxed and eating right, so it is good for you and the baby.

On this last point, as the week wore on, the father quipped that it was like a boring hospital resort vacation for the mom. The cost they were told would be around $160/RMB 1,000 per day inclusive.

They inquired further, "Is this really necessary?" The answer was, "No, it is not, but it is highly recommended to be most safe and supportive of mom and baby's health."

Upon hearing this recommendation, the expat couple sought a third opinion and was introduced through a close friend to an experienced maternity specialist at one of Shanghai's very expensive international hospitals for corporate expats with employee package health insurance coverage. That person was a highly intelligent, native Chinese who also spoke fluent English and she offered the following admonishment:

"This is the classic way of doing things in the Chinese maternity hospital system. You are stuck in it. There is no proof that giving amino acids and vitamins via IV to the mother is any help at all."

There was an additional issue. The timing of the birth fell right in the middle of the October holiday period when many people including doctors are on holiday. Therefore, we were further warned:

"They will surely push you to set a date to have a C-section before the holiday starts. I guarantee it. That's what 'they' will do."

That encouragement of a C-section never happened. From the beginning, the couple expressed a desire to have a natural child birth and the hospital made it clear as day that they were more than happy to support a natural childbirth. They would only recommend or insist on a C-section if it was needed due to a health complication. On this point, it is meaningful to mention that many Chinese women have C-sections even when they don't actually *need* one. They often choose in advance the specific birth date for auspicious reasons or convenience for mothers who also happen to have careers. In fact, in Shanghai there is one particular hospital located in Jinqiao that is well known for having a high rate of C-sections and the Chinese moms who choose to have a C-section in advance often use that hospital. As Chinese are known behaviorally and culturally for their pragmatic approach, this characterization well fits the profile of Chinese society. In America and other countries, there is also ongoing controversy that there are too many unnecessary C-sections, but perhaps driven by a different set of values and reasons. In both the United States and China, more revenue and profit for hospitals and doctors has been well-documented as influential drivers leading to too many C-section procedures.

Approximately three weeks after her recommended "hospital support vacation holiday week," the mother gave birth to a healthy baby boy weighing in at 2.6 kg/6 lbs., right at the lower range of the birth weight standard. The couple was as satisfied as all the other couples and, in addition, was quite glad that they had agreed to the added attention and $1,000 expense of mom-to-be's extra week's care.

On the day of the birth, the couple went into the hospital for a final check on a Thursday. The doctor had told the mom to do so if she had not yet gone into labor. Upon arrival, mom-to-be was checked into a semi-private room, which by luck did not have another expectant mom in the other bed. It was suggested that to induce labor, they would break her water and check the fluid to insure it was healthy. If not, they would let us know and discuss whether or not to have a C-section. As it turns out, the placenta liquid was fine and the labor process began shortly thereafter. Dad never had time to pick up the Baldacci novel he had brought along expecting a commonly twelve-hour birth ordeal. This particular mom wowed the crowd despite her very petite frame, revealing herself to be a true champion baby maker; she experienced a fast, steady, four-hour labor from 1 p.m. until 5 p.m. and gave natural birth at 5:30 p.m. Dad cut the umbilical cord with tears and awe, and baby was swept away for about 30 minutes by the attending nurses who diligently went about their business of checking and cleaning the newborn boy while over-the-moon new Dad comforted his exhausted, tearfully elated wife. The nurses returned the baby boy to mom's waiting arms for a few minutes before then transferring her back up to her hospital bed.

It was one of the finest days of this author's life and we named him Vincent Louis.

The name Vincent honors my family's Italian heritage through my great aunt Vincenzina who lived to be 101 and the name Louis honors my wife's Chinese family name by similar pronunciation, which is Liu.

Post-birth care by the nurses was as diligent as one might expect. A hospital-arranged photographer came by to take complimentary photos for the new parents and of course, left a business card behind for future family photo sessions. A nurse came by regularly to check on mom and baby and to teach this couple how to handle, feed, clean, and diaper our little Vincent Louis. We were given thorough explanation of what to expect and what to look for as any problems may seem to appear.

In the interest of fairness and remembering that this quality experience is a composite of the experiences of eight couples, let's ask how it could have been worse. What could have gone wrong? We do know that three of the couples had C-sections. One by choice, while the other two moms had tried and failed to do a natural birth. They were exhausted and after several hours, they went ahead with a C-section. One of the moms who gave natural childbirth had an epidural for pain relief.

With respect to the experiences of other couples, we have heard secondhand horror stories of bad medical care and I am sure they happen and I quickly deduce they are indeed unfortunate, and are the exception, not the rule. I am told of one such story at the local hospital of third-tier city Sanya in Hainan, that when the doctors did a C-section, they did it without anesthesia, that the mother was tortured by this and still freaked out about it, but I could not be told any detail about how severe the emergency was that a doctor might choose to do that rather than to anesthetize first no matter what. Would that ever happen in America or Europe? I am certain we can all assume that at local, lower-level hospitals throughout the world including China, the care and hygiene is not of such high standards, that such hospital locations across more rural areas have a lower standard of equipment and doctor's expertise to deal with complicated situations. I have been to many such local hospitals in China and they don't inspire any confidence to say the least. The experience of our couples in this story well represents the state of the familiar first--tier hospitals located throughout China's urban cities.

Why is this story part of the Big Lie? Because while on the very important subject of healthcare delivery in China, let's take a moment to note that common medical expenses in China are dirt-cheap compared to the United States, even without health insurance. A typical visit to the hospital costs $2 to see a doctor for your ailment; cheap antibiotic prices such as $5 for Zithromax, Cipro, Cefaclor; $10 for X-rays; $10 for various blood tests; $50 for a CAT scan; and $150 for an MRI. Foreign friends I know have had very satisfactory hernia operations for no more than $1,500, all inclusive. In contrast, lower- and middle-class Americans now face health care costs that have spiraled to the moon and beyond. Regardless of whether or not and how the current Obamacare battle may have an impact, families can ill afford hundreds of dollars per month in health care premiums with high deductibles and co-pays. This state of affairs providing reasonable, efficient healthcare at extremely low cost speaks volumes as to how a similar Chinese family is able to save hundreds of dollars more in their bank account each month. Multiply that over the past ten years and we have a picture of hundreds of billions of dollars that have remained in the hands of families broadly across society, not in the profit coffers of behemoth healthcare, pharmaceutical, and insurance companies paying their CEOs five million plus per year.

There is a final, fascinating story to consider regarding our long-time friend who is a local Chinese doctor stationed at the local Rui Jin #1 Hospital in Shanghai and whom we have trusted for years. When we wish to see her at Rui Jin Hospital, the registration fee at the window is around three dollars, the cost of an ultrasound RMB 50 (US$9), a CT scan RMB 350 (US$60), standard blood-test panel RMB 200 (US$30), acupuncture treatment RMB 50 (US$8). But then we know that this same doctor and many others also works at one of the branded international hospitals in the afternoons, where the cost of an appointment is around $100, and the cost of the exact same medical services is triple what I listed. But of course, the expats' insurance package covers those outrageously inflated fees, which are billed to an insurance company. Hmm.

Story VII: Mr. Yang's Dumplings

Several years ago until the new urban development came along, Wujiang Lu was a typical, shoddy, local restaurant street just off of Nanjing Xi Lu in the heart of Shanghai. Wujiang Lu is one of many similar streets throughout China where often the space of a restaurant vendor is just a few square shoddy meters with equally few, rickety chairs and plastic stools to sit and eat. The food is freshly prepared daily and often quite tasty.

One such shoddy restaurant shack along Wujiang Lu was the original location of "Yang's Dumplings" in Chinese-known "Xiao Yang Shen Jian," which serves pork-filled dumplings fried crispy on one side only in a big, round, flat, cast-iron pan. Mr. Yang's shack seemed to have a perpetual line of customers seven days a week and my friend Jeff recalls the day he decided to sit across from Yang's shoddy shack to actually count how many orders went out in an hour's time. His count was around 300. Back to Sherlock's use of deductive reasoning and calculation, I safely conclude that Mr. Yang's dumplings sells at least 1,000 orders per day seven days per week at RMB 4 or US$0.75 per order. That revenue totals RMB 120,000 or US$20,000 per month. The space was no larger than 15 square feet, so the rent could not possibly be more than $750–$1,500 per month and the cost to pay six full-time employees at $300 per month each equals $1,800. Finally, we assume a standard 30% food cost; add up all those easily recognized expenses to less than $10,000 per month, leaving at least $10,000 per month in profit, year after year. A hole-in-the-wall raking in over six figures a year.

Not, I gather, what most of us were thinking when first pondering a tiny, old, hole-in-the-wall dumpling joint of which similar hundreds of thousands of dumpling and noodle shops are scattered all over the country. Let's also be mindful that in terms of daily work lifestyle, all may not be wine and roses for such businesses that are part of China's street merchant economy.

Story VIII. Mr. & Mrs. Yang

Meet Mr. & Mrs. Yang, they've been quietly, simply, diligently making a daily profit of 1000rmb/USD $165 per day five days a week for over a decade, not a dime of it reported to the government. Now wash, rinse, repeat millions of times along China's merchant-lined streets to finally have an understanding of what's really going on in China.

This story is unique in that I first met the Yang's in 2002 when I lived in the Jing An district of Shanghai and regularly stopped at their "hole in the wall" street spot to pick up a 10rmb/$1.50 order of their tasty "jiaoyan de" chicken tenders, tossed with fresh minced garlic, green onion and chili peppers. I had moved away from my Jing An neighborhood apartment to live in several other locations of Shanghai since then and having a new corporate client in the same neighborhood this year, I found them still there; same spot, same business, probably the same old iron wok too. It is eleven years later and I always stop by their place to pick up an order when I'm in the neighborhood.

Having a long time friendship and trust with them, I inquired in a friendly conversation with the Yang's last week that went like this:

Mario: "So, Mrs. Yang, how many of these chicken tender orders are selling each day, 200 or more?"

Mrs. Yang: "At least…200 to 250 on average, sometimes 300."

Mario: "Nice! Your cost is around 50%?...profit around 5rmb each?... that's not bad."

Mrs. Yang: "No, no, only 3rmb profit ($.50) per order, look at the other expenses, the gas, the oil, it adds up, and we don't want to charge too much. And don't forget we also sell these whole chickens at around 20rmb each, we sell 50/day and make 5rmb profit on those."

So there you have it plain as day, right under your nose and every other cliche we might consider with respect to a China reality check. 250 x 3rmb = 750rmb plus 50 x 5rmb = 250rmb totaling 1000rmb per day profit. The funny thing is I sense that many of us perhaps were thinking that their total revenue per day was around that 1000rmb per day. Now, having done plenty of similar street side research in the past two years, their answer was right in line with what I expected. They are in fact taking in 3x more revenue and profit than most people might consider.

Keeping in mind the other stories so far and that this simple story has its start over a decade earlier, one might begin to imagine how much money they have diligently accumulated over the years.

Story IX. Mr. Cheng's BBQ Chicken Necks

Mr. Cheng is out on the street nightly barbecuing freshly the tastiest marinated chicken necks you've ever had. A tasty alternative to the more popular chicken wings but that's not the focus of our story here. Mr. Cheng lives in the district neighborhood of Shenyang in northern China, known as 205 or "Er Ling Wu" in Mandarin. That's all you have to say to a cab driver in Shenyang whereupon he knows exactly where to go. It's perhaps akin to saying "Little Italy" to a cabdriver in Manhattan. This happens to be my mother in law's long time neighborhood, one of Shenyang's original city neighborhoods with 15-20 year old apartment complexes, slowly being revitalized including the opening of the local subway station along the city's first subway line, about a ten minutes walk down the road. So it won't surprise to learn that I personally know many of the locals, literally being the only foreigner with a reason to visit such a local spot in the city. We frequently pop downstairs to hang out and eat street side ordering from the many street vendors who open their portable food carts each evening. The food is cheap, freshly prepared daily, cooked right in front of you and we find this scenario typical of evening street life all across China.

However, guilty of not paying close enough attention to how our unconscious mind filters millions of bits of information every second in discerning our view of reality, we have to stop and face some false assumptions. We observe that the street side areas of China are relatively dirty, the portable food carts are often worn and rickety while the novice tourist wouldn't dare to eat street food due to concerns about hygiene and food handling practices. Finally, the vendors themselves, well, they look just like down to earth street people. Many of them appear poor, even disheveled, as we would expect hard working street merchants just trying to "make ends meet" might look.

For many, such lack of perfection and pomp is part of the charm. Now I must briefly shift your attention dear reader to a grammatical point, to telling you that I hate the word "but", avoiding it like an annoying mosquito in most every communication circumstance.

But…

I figure Mr. Cheng has at least $100,000 cash in the bank. Which just might mean; all the other vendors do too.

Guilty once again of friendly, inquisitive chitchat with local friends based on my more personal relationship with them, I can inform you that Mr. Cheng sells around 300 necks/day 7 days/week at 2.5rmb/$.38 cents each, with a food cost of 1rmb/$.12 per neck. Yes, I checked with my mother in law; fresh daily chicken necks run around 20 at 20rmb per "jin" which is 1.1 lbs. at the local farmer's market.

Mr. Cheng's grill grosses an estimated 750RMB/$125 per day off the books cash and nets 450rmb/$75 per day, while a minimum wage retail/restaurant employee in America nets about $50 after taxes. He also sells the leg/thigh piece. So he's likely putting $1000/month for heaven knows how long in the bank. Let me take an extra moment to emphasize why that is a very realistic estimate; households like Mr. Cheng's have extremely low daily living expenses. They live in an apartment they likely own and for which they originally paid no more than $10,000. He has for all these years had no mortgage, no property taxes, and extremely low daily household expenses. He has no car payment and related expenses unless he recently bought a car and if he did buy a car, 80% of such car buyers pay cash, so he likely has no monthly car payment. Even if he is an official registered street vendor with a $200 annual business license, his business is all cash and we can be confident he far underreports his actual nightly take so his tax bite is minimal. Nobody asks for a "receipt please" on the merchant streets of China and you sure as heck won't find a placard on stuck on his cart with "If we fail to give you a receipt, your meal is free".

Mr. Cheng, according to our hard-working unconscious filtering, is a beneath- us, uneducated street merchant in the lower income class selling food on the street desperate to make ends meet.

We would never have considered that he has over $100,000 in the bank and has made it by more or less legitimate means, by toiling plainly and steadily over many years. More so, his money does not officially exist as he is simply one of millions across China's streets doing the same to the tune of trillions in the off the books cash economy. Side by side in this particular neighborhood block, in addition to the many local restaurants found in the actual building rows, there are around 40 merchants doing the same thing every night with their own portable food carts. Do the police come around? I suppose they do. And I suppose they like chicken necks.

Defining the "Big Lie" More Precisely

Chinese people are doing much, much better than you know, they don't want you to really know, and that's how they like it, even with each other. They live daily in a widespread, off-the-books cash economy of $6 to $10 trillion US dollars, unheard of in the United States, where credit card plastic is encouraged to track your every purchase, where the IRS is a diligent, fire-breathing dragon on every dime you earn and spend, and where the cash economy hovers at only around $2 trillion.

There are at least 100 million lower and middle-class Chinese citizens whose lives are exactly the same as those in the real-life stories I have shared with you. They possess somewhere in the range of $20,000 to $100,000 to even $500,000 US dollars cash that no one officially knows they actually have. This is the silent, unspoken secret that is no secret at all to the common Chinese citizen, for whom this is simply a way of life in a society in which most would not imagine it being any other way. They do not let anyone know, including each other, how well they actually are doing. They are very private about their true state of affairs. They hide what they do have.

Chinese have far more than you know and are doing far better than the other person knows and will never know because they will not ever tell; not you, not each other, or anyone who is not directly associated with the need to know. They do not reveal what does not supposedly exist, which are the trillions in cash in the unofficial economy that everyone knows does exist because it is everywhere. Follow me when I articulate it is cash, used to live, to consume, and to invest to make more cash in the unofficial, unreported economy of trillions which exists; ergo, it does not exist and they don't reveal it except in its use. This idea may also help you to now realize the nature of many seemingly unwise, unprofitable, commercial projects embarked upon; a component of their function is to create vehicles to park or distribute the massive cash spoils sloshing around amongst China's tight relationship circles of business and friendship, often known as their "guanxi" relationships.

The citizens of Chinese society engage in such value-driven behavior quietly and in a clever, unassuming manner. It is perfectly normal, reasonable, and unconscious behavior to a Chinese person to behave this way; as normal and reasonable as it feels for a pregnant, European woman to drink one glass of red wine per day, or friendly small-town American strangers to offer each other a smiling "Good Morning!" as they pass along the road—both normal behaviors in those cultures, which a typical Chinese would rarely engage in their culture.

In the myriad types of business negotiations that exist, ranging from buying a T-shirt at the local flea market to investing in a major infrastructure project, they will equally not show their hand but force you to show yours. When you go street shopping at a Chinese flea market, notice a jacket you like, and ask, "How much is this?" they will instead ask you to tell them first. "How much do you want to pay?" is often the reply, as unbelievable as that may seem. This is a classic "art of war" negotiating tactic, to cause the opponent to reveal their hand first while not yet revealing your own. In business negotiations a common post-negotiation complaint is that the Chinese side didn't "lie," they just didn't reveal. Ahh, yes, now you're getting it.

While this is individual behavior, it is sociologically speaking also behavior that characterizes their collective conscious, and therefore as a country, it is exactly how they wish other nations to perceive their country. In America it is painfully well known that the rich are richer than ever and that the lower/middle class are in worse shape financially than ever with their salaries flat since 1997. This is not an opinion; it is a transparent, measurable and known state of affairs by everyone's traceable bank account and credit card usage. Living in America, it is much harder and expensive to "go off the grid" like actress Darryl Hannah. There is no such state of affairs in China where the known is known to be the undetectable unknown and part of most people's lives is off the grid all the time. The Chinese know what they don't know. It's a giant, normal secret. Have fun wrapping your head around that.

I suggest that while the Chinese government discloses, as expected, the more obvious dismal economic indicators, such as the high level of loans and potential defaults, they keep the good stuff going on close to the vest. They tell you publicly what you expect them to say not what may really be going on. This is simply good public relations strategy and practice and is widespread practice amongst many governments and large companies across the world under the guidance of the world's top PR firms who are the spin masters of messaging.

You recognize by now that I lean far toward believing that China is in much better shape than they want anyone to know rather than in much worse shape than they want anyone to know, while it seems the opposite is true of the United States often accused of not wanting us to know how bad things really are for the middle-lower and middle classes there. While outsiders misguidedly fret and frown and predict some version of China's woes, such views are based on the information China has allowed them to see while the tidal wave of quiet riches, investment, and colonialization is steadily reaching the shores of other continents at a fervent pace and scope far higher than any outsider realizes. While I can easily see through much of author Peter Navarro's inflammatory and flawed narratives against China, he is right to point out America should be worried about the direction of developing outcomes and balance of power.

Examining the magnitude of China's foreign outbound investment across the world begins to let you in on the reality of such matters, which outsiders would otherwise not consider. Throughout this book, I have included many such examples and cases to confirm this view, which includes many large-cap corporate, political, and government interests.

China is doing great, you don't know it and they like it that way. They withhold, they don't reveal—this is de facto behavior in this culture. One of my close colleagues who is Shanghainese reviewed this book. His feedback was, "You aren't describing anything I don't already know, it's right on the mark."

We must now step forward to examine, to deduce the underlying causes, the why of it all, and other matters related. In the parlance of modern corporate language, what are the underlying values and behavioral drivers leading to and behind such sociological phenomenon?

Chinese think and behave this way for the following reasons:

1. As a matter of privacy. Privacy of affairs and finances is highly valued.

2. As an expression of humility and quietness espoused by Confucian ideals and virtues of good character. They are less influenced by the characteristically absolute, puritanical rules of behavior often found in cultures with a stronger Judeo-Christian presence.

3. As a matter of self-protection since the woes they had experienced during the Cultural Revolution. Hence, the "Big Lie" is closely tied to the small-group, self-protective "guanxi" that you may be familiar with. (If you don't know, "guanxi" refers to the key relationships in your life, "who you know" to be able to get something done that otherwise is more difficult to do.

4. As a matter of survival and support. Indeed, if someone else knows I am doing well, they may have a number of reasons to come after me and take some of what I have.

5. As a tactical matter of not showing one's hand in business negotiations.

Speaking Of…

Chinese families and professionals who look poor on the outside often possess far more wealth beyond surface appearances. This is an ever-present behavioral mindset woven deeply into the neural pathways and emotional makeup of their individual behavior since childhood. This is a description of a specific well-formed society.

I speak of what appear to you as low-income families routinely growing their vegetables in whatever land might be available around their apartment, and so foregoing the Western $500-per-month grocery budget.

I speak to you of the Chinese businessman who once said to me, "Our low salaries? That is only a small part of what we do to make money."

I speak to you of businessmen who have unknown millions, who are negotiating with you as if they don't. In fact, the millions they possess are none of your damn business.

I speak of the Chinese government, which does not talk much about the obviously known shadow cash economy and leads to the dilemma and joys of its integral existence; invisible, untraceable, unknown, 100% hiding in plain sight. The joy of it is that the cash keeps the domestic economy as a well-oiled machine. The dilemma is the government not being able to collect much-needed billions in income taxes to support the fiscal budget needs of a massive, expanding country.

I speak of our neighbor Mrs. Yan, who looks like a frumpy, old, retired, local Shanghainese, who we estimate earns around US$3,000 per month cash by selling her egg pancake breakfasts for $0.75 every morning on the street leading to the subway stop.

I speak of sales people and bartenders on low salaries, and therefore who's expected, normal behavior is to get a kickback from the beverage supplier.

Then we naturally look to the restaurant's owner who won't bother firing the bartender because he knows the next bartender will do the same thing.

The restaurant owner used to be the bartender. That's how he made enough money to become the restaurant owner.

You knew that was coming.

I speak of suppliers who are more than happy to pay the kickbacks to the customer's manager in order to get the business.

I speak of people who take care of each other, who do business with each other in professional services as alumni together from the same school. One lady becomes an HR manager for a multinational, while her friend registers a small corporate training company. The owner of the training company kicks back part of the training contract to her friend the HR manager. The job gets done, the requirement gets fulfilled, but now you understand why another company putting in a bid never gets it. It's definitely not fair, boohoo.

I was recently told by the Director of Sales & Marketing for the meetings/events department of a well-known, five-star, luxury hotel chain brand that up to 30% of the quoted monies involved in a big promotional event in their hotel ballroom is slush between the various vendors, passed around between the various middlemen and decision-makers who enabled the players to play.

I speak of a Canadian I know who a few years ago helped a foreign affairs office of Anycity, China, to put together a planned international business conference. He edited the English translation and even made some suggestions to them on how to do things, sharing his ideas as to how things were done back in the West. They paid him $500 cash at $25/hour for the 20 hours he put in helping them. On the day he went to enjoy a post-event lunch with the event team and to be paid, he sat in the government office and watched the manager open the safe to reveal stacks of cash, of which he received his payment. Work was done, everyone was doing their job, the event was a success, and that was that. Just another day of doing business to get things done.

I speak of a Mr. Wang, Vice Director of the office of municipal business development or some such title, Anytown, China, who wears a suit, whose job is to attract and develop business, a nice position to be in, but again, with a salary of US$400, a wife and a young daughter. So when he befriends you and confides, "I'm looking for other business ventures, to work part-time, like a sales rep," is that such a surprise? Does it seem so unethical to pay someone a referral commission as a thank you for helping your business be successful?

Now let me ask you a question. If you and everyone around you were on a ridiculously low salary, wouldn't you try to figure out ways to "help each other out to make more money"? "Of course!" is the obvious, troublesome, conflict-ridden answer. When you live in a developed Western country where the wage for such a position is $3,000 to $6,000 per month, it is easy to say that shouldn't happen. But if everyone across the country was doing the same job for a pittance, you can quite easily recognize the paradigm shift and rationalizations that emerge.

I speak of Sunny, a Chinese gal from Luzhou who in 2005 invited her boyfriend to visit her family and friends on the prospect of a nice marriage. She told him, "All my friends are simple, average people, but they are very rich and you'd never know." It turns out one of them was running a local Chinese mobile phone business, the other was in telecom services, another had the factory making telecom industry related parts. They, indeed, were all quietly just living their simple lives, and quietly wealthy. They all owned their apartments mortgage free (easy to do when a nice apartment had only cost $30,000 back then). The boyfriend enjoyed with all her friends a typical, delicious meal in a local restaurant that didn't cost more than $10/head and afterwards they all played cards and drank $1 beers all night long. That's it. The simple, quiet life, with simple, quiet wealth.

I speak of a five-star international hotel retail store manager who didn't even want or ask for a kickback, yet still was given a $500 red envelope with genuine gratitude from the construction vendor who was involved in the opening of the retail shop.

I speak of a talented, attractive, 24-year-old Chinese woman who works as a TV show host for the Shanghai TV station earning only $25 per show. Yet, she is paid $2,500 when hired as the bilingual emcee for corporate conferences and meetings in the MICE industry several times per year. This is similar to how celebrities and actors make a large portion of their money: not from the shows they are in or the sports team they perform on, but the secondary endorsements and other business activities that bring in the bulk of their income.

It's so simple and so obvious, that's why we miss it.

The Chinese behavior to keep quiet about what you are doing, to not show your hand, to not reveal to your counterpart in a negotiation, to be humble, creates a value system that exactly would drive and support this type of behavior and cause a cash economy to flourish, as indeed it has in Chinese society.

Meet Professor Wang and Credit Suisse

I am aware that in 2010 Credit Suisse published a report on the subject of China's hidden economy. The report was in cooperation with Professor Wang Xiaolu of the China Reform Foundation who is best known for his work on the subject of China's shadow economy. Based on Professor Wang's survey correlating income and spending patterns, it seems the conclusion is that urban per-capita disposable income of Chinese households should be RMB 32,154, which is 90% above the official data. And that conclusion was reached back in 2008, not in 2013 when China' expansion has an additional five years under its belt.

According to China's National Statistics Bureau, China's affordability ratio in 2010 was 8:1, significantly higher than a country such as the US. However, Dr. Wang concludes, if we factor in China's grey market economy, China's national affordability ratio drops in half to 4:1, which is similar to that in the US. Surely this is reasonable; as we lop off health insurance premiums, car payments, credit card debt payments, and property taxes off anyone's middle-class budget, we've just improved cash in hand by well over $1,000 per month.

Outside of this book, this work by Dr. Wang with Credit Suisse is the only official research I have found on the subject to date. My view is that the ongoing societal and economic development that has taken place in China since the 2008–10 period has led to an even greater degree of financial freedom and lifestyle amongst China's middle classes. Any HR consulting organization such as Hewitt will inform you that all salaries—especially white-collar salaries—continue to rise to Western levels, a thorn in the side of companies who came to China for the low labor cost advantages relative to the West.

Over the past five years through 2013, we have witnessed a continued boom in domestic consumer spending, still averaging growth of over 12% per year according to reported statistics and not hard to believe standing here on the local streets. Yet, whether China's current government leadership can successfully navigate the transition away from infrastructure and real estate development with greater reliance on domestic consumer spending and its rising import demand remains to be seen.

Meanwhile, one thing we know for sure, the nouveau riche middle classes of China absolutely love their cars.

Oh, Dear! They Have a Car Loan!

Our discourse also explains a typical conversation with a Chinese in which they ask direct questions such as, "Do you have a loan on your new car?" If you answer yes, they wonder what your problem is, why you didn't have enough cash to pay for the whole thing in the first place because they do. I am not speaking only of the rich people; I am speaking of the lower and middle class who are in the habit of paying for everything without credit. In fairness and to be realistic, as Chinese society has expanded and inflated, the percentage of common folks taking loans and mortgages is rising. Checking recently with several local car dealers including Buick, Peugeot, and Toyota, the salesman told me that around 20% of buyers were taking loans, typically on cars costing from US$20,000 to $35,000.

My formal definition of the "Big Lie" in case it would ever be included in Webster's Dictionary:

The "Big Lie": hiding, not stating to others how well one is really doing; such an attitude and value system pervasive and apparent in the mindset and culture of a given group of people inhabiting a given country.

I draw this chapter to a close with a paradoxical axiom often noted amongst foreigners living here:

"If you want to feel poor, come to China."

Parsing such a saying further, we are certainly referring to every working Chinese citizen or farmer, many of whom struggle, many of whom have no such opportunity to even get involved in ways to improve their lot in life. Hundreds of millions across China live with the stark reality that competition to survive is fierce and merciless as in many countries across the world. The main themes found in this book are centered on the 200–400 million members of China's rising urban middle classes.

1999: You're Going Where?

So, let's begin fourteen years ago, to explore the chain of events and as I would even say the fate that brought me to be in China now for nearly 13 years.

Early in 1999, I was sitting in my room at the SunJoy hotel in Chengdu, Sichuan Province, a few short blocks from the United States Consulate on a typically cloudless day when it hit me that I was not going to use my return ticket back to the United States the next day.

I loved the fact that there was a husband/wife–owned rat hole of a restaurant across the street serving generous plates of the most delicious, fresh, handmade pork-vegetable dumplings for closer to a dime than a dollar. I hated the fact that I hadn't seen even a glimpse of the sun for three months and would not for still another three. Juxtaposing these two extremes only begins to cause you to forget everything you think you know about a place like China.

Several months earlier in Los Angeles, my acupuncturist in Garden Grove had introduced me to Frank, a nice Chinese gentleman and entrepreneur living in the area. Like almost all Americans in 1998 and even today, China was a mysterious place hidden behind an iconic "wall," distinct from the other countries around the Pacific Rim and viewed in a singular, mostly negative manner.

For example, if you told your friends you were going to Japan, the Philippines, or Thailand, they would say "cool" or "that sounds great"; their questions would betray their genuine interest in your pending expedition. But when informed of my intention to go to China, the reaction of my friends was far more emotional and demonstratively negative, along the lines of:

"Huh?"

"You're kidding."

"What the hell are you doin' that for?"

"Wow, geez, aren't they a bunch of Commies?"

"You better be careful, you might never get out."

While on our first flight across the Pacific, which was in fact like far too many Americans my first adventure off the continent, Frank declared the obvious cliché,

"Forget everything you think you know or ever heard about China."

Frank was dead right, easily proving why such statements become cliché. And I was in a personal situation that prepared me to forget everything and be open to new experiences—a new chapter or, as it turned out, a new volume of my life.

Frank's family was originally from Chongqing, the world's largest city with a population of about 30 million people (including the suburban and satellite communities of the metropolitan area).

When he invited me to come to China, I had been living in Los Angeles for three years, starting my life over post-divorce. While it was doubtless the most difficult period of my life, it was also, thankfully, a period during which I learned hard and valuable life lessons for the future.

I mention this to make a point; if you had suggested to me at that time that in my immediate future I would be half way around the world eating delicious chicken feet and duck tongues in a city that dwarfs L.A., all of whose residents were much shorter than me, who were incessantly staring at me and with whom I could barely communicate, I'd have said you were nuts.

Yet, there I was, sitting on my hotel bed, of sound mind, deciding to stay as I said to Frank, "I'm not leaving, I'm not using my return ticket, I'm renting a local apartment." I would say that the freshness of God's cosmic 2x4 whacking me across the head trumped whatever hardships and fears I was facing.

There were two key reasons behind my decision, both of which seemed practical enough at the time. First, I was simply enjoying the emotional freshness of this journey; the inherent value of being smacked by that cosmic force, being immersed in a radically different culture, environment, and mindset.

The awakening was shocking. It was rejuvenating and invigorating. It was exhausting and frightening. It forced new levels of transforming awareness, of thought streams like, "Whoa, right and wrong here make absolutely no sense."

Secondly, since my youth I'd always had a "wanderlust" unlike many of my American contemporaries: that undeniable compulsion to go abroad, to check out what it was like to live in other cultures, to feel it, not read about it or watch it—to experience it!

In 1999, China, after interminable negotiations, was set to finally gain entry into the World Trade Organization. This was not just a watershed for that country, for international trade, for government relations. It was my break too, the fissure that allowed me to breach the Great Wall. I could see it clearly. I could feel it in the air. I had done the research. I believed my background as a professional speaker and trainer was enough to go on and I was soon invited by the US Consulate to speak at a series of conferences in Western China organized by their Foreign Commercial Service division, along with Sichuan Ministry of Foreign Trade and Economic Cooperation (MOFTEC), and the Chengdu Foreign Affairs Department of the Sichuan government. I also acted as the representative of a group of investors interested in doing business in China. The venture never did produce a profit, which was not exactly surprising under the conditions. You might now ask: what conditions?

"How can you start a venture when there are no rules in place?" I wondered.

For example, there had been a large new dental practice operating in nearby Guizhou Province for over a year without any kind of business licenses. Why? Because no mechanisms even existed within the bureaucracy to regulate the licensing and launch of such an enterprise.

It was a treacherous entrepreneurial journey strewn with endless vagaries, direct and indirect payoffs, and circular, pointless negotiations that would make the most patient negotiators in the world want to cry, commit murder, or throw in the towel and go home. And due to the lack of codified regulations and transparency, future operations could never be assured.

The rules of the game could be changed without notice. No did not mean no, not in business any more than in the pursuit of women. Hissing air between teeth, on the other hand, accompanied by calm declarations that something you wanted was "inconvenient"—now that definitely meant no! But you, of course, being the idiot foreigner, spent the next several weeks, even months thinking the deal was still alive.

That is how my incredibly diverse journey and education began and there have been some great experiences along the way. In many ways—now that I have a reputation as an accomplished professional speaker and advisor, I have visual recognition from appearances in a popular Chinese mini-series with Hong Kong superstar Zhen Zhe Wei, I am a culture show host for Shanghai TV in one of the most repeated New Year advertisements, I work with Korea's top music stars to promote the international Korean conglomerate Lotte, and I have performed jazz in venues around the country—it seems a lifetime ago.

Jim Rogers is a popular investment guru; he is the creator of the Rogers International Commodities Index and author of the book, *Investment Biker: Around the World with Jim Rogers*. I invoke his name because with respect to China, he made one of the most insightful and poignant comparisons of economic development in the world, which tells us the story most eloquently:

"If you were smart in 1807 you moved to London, if you were smart in 1907 you moved to New York City, and if you are smart in 2007 you move to Asia."

Of course while Jim does not specify beyond "Asia" in this quotation, he is very much aware that China is the "head of the dragon," the rising market powerhouse and leader of Asia. His belief is so strong that he is making sure his children learn Mandarin.

My own experience over the past dozen years living in China has made it possible for me to confirm that the words of Jim Rogers and my friend Frank from Chongqing are spot on.

Ancient Teachings: Cats, Prozac, and Road Rage

Fabulous stuff to ponder, the teachings of the ancients; the Egyptians, the Greeks, Jesus, Buddha, name your guru.

Be as a child, not like a child, said Jesus.

The purity and innocence and curiosity and zest we find in a child symbolizes the sweet, effortless side of life, of existence. Lilies in the field don't do anything. They just "be" lilies. Birds just "be" birds, doing what they naturally do. And wouldn't it be silly if the fish asked, "Excuse me, where is the ocean?" It is simply aware and exists and doesn't need to question the pervasive sense of well-being it has. Well, at least not until a bigger fish comes along and tries to have it for a meal.

And cats, let's not forget cats. Wouldn't you love to be a cat? If you revealed such a longing to your American psychologist they'd suggest switching your meds from Prozac to Zoloft.

Meanwhile, in China, most people have much tougher challenges to their daily lives with a lower standard of living, yet there's hardly a psychologist or psychiatrist or AA meeting to be found!

So, in contrast to the Prozac nation, how do they cope with the onslaught of life's mental, emotional, and physical challenges without the billions of dollars worth of anti-depressants and professional counseling being hawked on TV in the West?

Confucius Says: No Road Rage

In China people drive like lunatics, but they never get upset while driving. Mostly, they ignore each other like emotionless robots. (I did say mostly because there are flare-up fights, which become a public spectacle yet fortunately don't ever include guns.) This behavior is rooted in Confucian ethics, not the Bible's golden rule to do unto others, but simply, "Don't show your emotions, it means you have weak character." We can recognize in their behavior a root of pragmatic, mental discipline coupled with emotions in check. Understanding that the traditional "pass the exam" Chinese school system, infused with such Confucian principles, also helps us to identify with where this sort of behavioral discipline has its roots.

Conversely, when I was in Italy to attend the Umbria Jazz Festival in 2006, we passengers watched our Roman airport van driver spend an eternity leaning out the window screaming and cursing at another driver for an almost imperceptible transgression. At each red traffic light, he hung his head out the window and started. When the light turned green he stopped and when the light turned red he started again. "Follow us to the airport!" he howled in passionate Italian. "After I drop them off, I'll kick your ass, follow me to Fumicino airport!"

In America, the insult of honking your horn for five seconds too long can result in another driver getting out of their car, possibly with a gun and confronting you for being rude.

Moreover, last year I had a Phoenix cop pull me over and tell me during his authoritative diatribe that he could and should give me a ticket for "misuse of my horn." The land of the free, eh?

I have to listen to misguided Americans tell me how little freedom Chinese supposedly have and then I find this kind of ridiculous intrusion and law in the daily life of a "free" American?

Speaking of cars, in China, horn honking is constant; it is expected and accepted. (Note: big cities in recent years have begun "no honking" policies in the interest of peace and quiet.) All these contrasting behaviors, rules, expectations, and norms are not constant—in different families, in different environments, in different cultures the rules are re-written and we must allow this diversity to serve as a reminder not to be absolute judges of right and wrong by our own limited sense of ethics and moral code.

Politeness, Etiquette, and Ritual

If there ever was a topic where an understanding of context was necessary, politeness and etiquette are it. Codes of etiquette and values can differ widely in Chinese culture compared with the rest of the world.

The American concept of "right and wrong" tends to be defined in absolute terms regardless of the parameters; the same notion in Chinese culture tends to be a more nuanced "depends on the situation" approach.

Consider the following dichotomy:

To an American, many Chinese people show a glaring lack of politeness and good manners in situations where such graces are to be expected. At the same time, the Chinese may appear to go overboard on politeness in situations where an American would put little value in such a demonstration of kindness.

Kiss Kiss, Hug Hug

Drawing the lines of expression of affection is a fascinating subject across cultures. When I meet and greet my French friends, male or female, even though I am a typical Italian American, we embrace and give each other two rather soft, genuine kisses, one on each cheek.

If it's with folks from Eastern Europe, we go back around to the other side for a third kiss! More importantly is that in the context of that expression, the feeling is genuine and nice.

When two Americans meet up, it can also be quite a friendly affair with hugs and pats, skipping the double cheek kiss kiss.

When Chinese family members haven't seen each other for six months they say, "Hello, happy to see, how are you?" and they don't touch each other or kiss or hug.

Yep, that's right.

Now here's where it gets interesting and I make a comparison to Italian culture. The Chinese will then "take action" to express their respect and happiness at being together again more so than is seen in other cultures.

They will go into the rituals of getting food and tea, literally running quickly around the house figuring out how to bend over backwards for you in some way, whether you want it or not, to make sure you truly understand that they are happy to be with you again.

Likewise in business offices, where Chinese employees engage in the behavior of rushing quickly to get what you have asked for, which I suggest is their version of attentive, customer service.

In other words, expression of feelings in Chinese culture is more by ongoing pragmatic action rather than brief affections. The Chinese wife of a foreign man, and I include this point with respect to my own marriage to my wife who is from Shenyang in northern China, will chide her husband to "stop saying I love you and *do* something to show it!"

A husband/wife spat in this marriage structure often ends much more quickly by the husband wisely keeping his mouth very shut, making soup, and then serving it to his still angry wife. Follow this with a couple of other "domestic acts" like tidying up the house and bingo, you're out of the dog house.

Affections, hugs, kisses, and "I love you's" are welcome too, but the domestic actions are tops on the totem pole of values in Chinese relationships to express that you care or to express apology.

Related to this behavior of expressing friendship in a more pragmatic way, Chinese will show up as a guest at someone else's home with fruit not flowers. One can quickly grasp that line of thinking; fruit is fresh and colorful and healthy and has utility as food, while flowers, no matter how pretty and colorful, will be dead in a week.

Tomato Soup Is Love

When, shall we say, an American boy is feeling miserable and sick, he needs mom. His mother holds him and pays attention to him and coos over him and feeds him a nice bowl of tomato soup.

Ahh, yes, feeling love and attention for that boy is . . . tomato soup.

When a Chinese little girl is feeling miserable and sick, she needs mom too. Her mom also holds her and pays attention to her and coos over her, prepares and feeds her steamed buns stuffed with a delicious sweet black sesame paste.

I know you get the point of the unconscious yet deep emotional associations we make, which come from our external environment and exert a powerful force on our personalities and behavior.

Inside Out, Upside Down, Arm in Arm

While I just finished telling you that China is a place where we find a dearth of affection and touching in family and friend greeting-type situations, in contrast, the arm in arm and hand-holding intimacy between male to male and female to female friends is refreshingly high.

Note that I am not referring to gay and lesbian relationships. It is not uncommon to find two young men walking along with one of them comfortably grasping an arm or with their arms casually dropped over the shoulder of their companion.

Likewise with females, it is commonplace to find two female friends walking along holding hands or arm in arm and there is absolutely nothing sexual about this behavior. You remember my friend Frank from Chongqing, right?

I easily recall the first time that he comfortably grasped my arm as we were walking along the street and beginning a particular conversation. It was a simple expression of friendship and trust and natural communication. Knowing that was the case in this cultural context, I accepted and appreciated the behavior for what it was.

Saying No or Hissing Your Teeth

In Asia, and especially China, people almost never say no. They hesitate, they smile, they remain silent, they hiss air through their teeth while shaking their head, they tell you it may be inconvenient, they tell you it's possible and do nothing for days, hoping you will get the hint, but they will *never say no*.

An American may think it is much better to cut to the chase; avoid wasting time; give a direct answer; move on. Such thinking simply does not exist in China because "no" is not polite. "Hey," the American says, "I don't need polite. I just need to know if the answer is yes or a no. Either one is fine, so long as you just please tell me."

If the "no" does happen, it is always accompanied by expressions of apology, embarrassment, and regret. But that's only if you ever get to the "no" in the first place.

It's hysterically funny to watch this mismatched cultural dance between a local and a recently arrived foreigner, especially those Americans who in particular think they know it all.

This tendency among Americans often manifests itself as arrogance when visiting "less developed" places—which, let's face it, to most Americans is anywhere beyond their own borders. Lest you think I am bashing Americans, I am not, because in fact, American society encourages and enables admirable levels of knowledge across life.

If you have a discussion with an American 12- to 16-year-old student and a Chinese 12- to 16-year-old student, the American teen demonstrates a far greater breadth and depth of knowledge about the world around them.

It's just that on this point with respect to business, that same breadth and depth of knowledge is insular to their life as an American, which then manifests itself as arrogance when outside their own borders.

Amazingly Tolerant

Behaviors that are often regarded as bothersome, completely intolerable, or annoying to the point of madness to an American are quietly taken in stride by a typical Chinese person.

For your edification I will explore the two most extreme and surprising of these behaviors in Chinese society. The first case has to do with a tolerance for noise. The second case involves driving habits.

Scene 1: Living in a Construction Zone

The most unbelievably annoying practice to touch the daily life of the ordinary resident of China, local or foreign, is home renovation. Apartments are bought as empty concrete shelters; basically a multi-floor network of caves. By all means, congratulations on the purchase of your new home! But in the interim . . .

From 6 a.m. until midnight, every day (in many cases including weekends and holidays), there will be hammering, drilling, pounding, sanding, and yelling until every unit has been bought and made livable by its owner. Any semblance of peace and quiet to which one may feel entitled outside the hours of midnight to 6 a.m. simply does not exist.

Imagine living within this scenario for the next three years without relief:

You and the other buyers purchase your new home in an apartment complex of 480 units. There are six buildings, 20 stories each, with four apartment units per floor.

While viewing your home, you hear the sounds of industrial drills, hammers, buzz saws, and jackhammers reverberating throughout the building, because every apartment is sold as an empty concrete shell and must be decorated.

Anything within five floors is what I call the intolerable zone. That is to say there are a total of 40 units—five floors above, five below—that are going to be decorated over the course of the next year or two and you are going to hear every pound of the hammer, every moment's buzz of the buzz saw, and every single miserable whining, whirring minute of the drills being driven into the concrete walls.

Because buildings in China are made of concrete, the vibrations carry much more efficiently into your living room, much louder than if a carpenter was drilling some wooden 2x4s not yet physically joined to the rest of the building.

There is no timetable set by the management company as to when the construction must be complete. So, while you may be thinking that everyone will complete the three-month process to decorate their homes in a state of joyful, neighborly togetherness and harmony, you are sadly mistaken.

In reality, three apartments plus your own will be decorated during the next 10–12 weeks. Assuming the unit has not been purchased purely as an investment for resale, in which case it may not be decorated until re-sold to someone who actually wants to occupy the space.

You will then bring in that fabulous new 52-inch flat screen and soft living room sofa, move in and start enjoying your happy new home. However, as construction on this set of apartments is wrapping up, two or three others will start up for the next two to three months, and as they are finishing up, three or four others will start up, still leaving well over 20 more units to be decorated in the next six months.

It gets worse. Imagine those other six 20-story buildings next to yours. Sound easily carries across the garden. Think of the almost subsonic rumbling vibration you can feel in the ground when a big truck drives by on the road downstairs.

The incessant construction sounds from those buildings are also constantly emanating from the apartments being decorated in those buildings too. Could the workers close the windows to keep the noise down? Don't be silly. The workers would suffocate in the dust.

This will go on for one year from 6 a.m. until midnight. I judge it as no less than misery, yet the Chinese simply accept and live with it because it is very important to them that they decorate their home from scratch, to make it truly their own.

It helps also to understand that during the past 20 years in China, there was not much of a market-driven resale market in real estate or anything else for that matter.

Recently, the more expensive apartment management offices have begun to be marginally stricter about limiting the times when construction work may be undertaken, making the situation relatively more bearable. The best-case scenario is living with the cacophony of construction sounds five days per week, 11 hours per day from 8 a.m. to 7 p.m., Monday through Friday; that's your veritable "Fortress of Solitude."

How can you rationalize this process of buying and decorating a home in China? I briefly alluded to the root motivation earlier. Elements of modern Chinese culture are still steeped in ancient tradition and superstition.

Concern about inheriting bad karma from previously decorated rooms, especially with regard to such an important purchase as a home, is simply not a risk worth taking. There is a general aversion to buying something "used" or "already built" by someone else, because you simply cannot be sure of the provenance. You don't want someone else's bad karma, right? For example, would you buy a home if you knew the previous owners were murdered in it?

Probably not. The Chinese extend this idea further into the karma of daily life. It is important to make your home "yours" from the ground up. Amen. Nice idea. Ergo the noise and why it's tolerated.

So you buy new or gut the second-hand apartment and put up with the noise when others do the same.

There is, however, another distinction worth making. They don't simply put up with the inconvenience of the noise; they accept the necessity of it. It is a part of their character as a society that I admire most in the sense that they accept and share the suffering of it together as a group. This practice is not going to come to an end in mainstream Chinese culture any time soon.

Scene 2: Headlight High Beam Experiment

Earlier in the recent boom in auto sales in China, my wife and I were based in Sanya, Hainan Province. This is a small "town," a fishing village in fact; not a sprawling urban metropolis by any stretch of the imagination. And it is a place where an incredible number of people drive their new Hondas, Toyotas, Nissans, BMWs, Mercedes, and Audis in the evening with their headlight high beams switched on.

I think I am safe in speaking for the majority of drivers when I say that driving into the high beam headlights of an oncoming car is blinding, annoying, and outright dangerous. My wife thinks I am nuts because I aggressively flash my high beams at the oncoming drivers to remind them to turn off their high beams. I confess, my success rate was alarmingly low.

This state of affairs remained the same for months on end until one day I was divinely inspired to do an experiment. Instead of thinking like a typical foreigner, I wondered what would happen if I did as the Romans, or in this case the Chinese. Be the Chinese driver!

I drove around the city for 30 minutes along the usual roads with my high beams *on*, ready with pen and paper to note how many times oncoming drivers would flash their lights at me.

Virtually no one did.

So, once again we have an example of widespread behavior in a society where people quietly tolerate what most of us in the West clearly regard as intolerable.

The Worst Drivers in the World Never Get Angry

The headlight high beam experiment is but one part of another surprising behavior pattern found in everyday Chinese life.

As I briefly touched on earlier in the chapter, driving habits and rules in China border on lunacy as far as a Westerner is concerned. Drivers routinely break the traffic law that Americans believe keep everyone safe. Let's look at few examples and then look more deeply at what is really going on behind the scenes to shape these behaviors. Here are a few examples:

Chinese drivers, including public buses, regularly weave across three full lanes, in and out of the marked lanes, often even into oncoming traffic. Everyone expects this type of behavior and thus no one is surprised or gets upset. And as you may be righteously ready to ask, "Doesn't a policeman stop the bus driver and give him a ticket?" This ain't Kansas, Dorothy.

The crosswalk light turns green for pedestrians to walk. Cars continue weaving through the intersection while pedestrians are crossing the street. It makes no difference whether the pedestrians are young, elderly, men, women, or children. Hard to believe.

When turning left, including through the pedestrians in the crosswalk from example #2, cars will cross from the far left to the inside lane, directly into lanes of oncoming traffic and then cut back over into the right lanes.

Think of the snake effect, when the whole line of cards slowly veers to the far left in an unbroken chain. Again, public buses do it too, often leading the way, as though it is a driver's perfect football linebacker leading the way to Vince Lombardi's daylight.

Drivers will slow to a crawl or stop in the middle of the road for no obvious reason. If they realize they are just about to miss their exit on the highway, they ignore safety; they *stop* in the far left lane of the expressway and figure out how to get across so as to not miss their exit, creating highly dangerous life-and-death situations on the highway.

They will not even think to pull over to the side so as not to impede traffic. They don't engage their hazard lights. They will often do this directly in the middle of an intersection.

Turning left at an intersection, the driver behind you does not follow directly behind you. He will cut to your left or right side turning left with your car.

The American Reaction

These driving habits would evoke a healthy dose of road rage in even the most docile American motorist. Regarded as no less than irresponsible, reckless endangerment by an idiot who obviously should not be allowed to drive, many good citizens would use their mobile phones to call the police to report the transgressions, while others may form a posse to encourage you to enroll in driver training.

If the police happened to see you first, you would not only receive a ticket. You would be arrested for such maneuvers; your license would be suspended, your auto insurance cancelled or jacked up to outrageous rates and you would most likely end up in jail or order to do hundreds of hours of community service.

Let me clearly state that every single righteous, outraged American who does call the police to report the dangerous idiot driver knows with zero doubt that they are 100% in the right. There is beauty and duty and honor in those ethics. But as individuals can we have enough awareness to recognize that those deeply held ethics are deeply integrated into the context in which they exist?

When in Rome, do as the Romans. Yes, right, that is absolutely right and reasonable!

Hmm, what am I up to in presenting such a worn cliché? Please, as you now allow yourself a moment to consider other extreme behavior; would your laundry service include having your clothes washed daily along with everyone else in a giant vat of freshly collected urine at the local laundromat?

Lunacy, yet in the days of the Roman Empire, that's exactly what they did, until they fortunately found better ways to get clothes clean and fresh.

Imagining the mom riding a bicycle with her child on the back weaving through the cars and busses, attempt to let yourself recognize it not as lunacy, but as the focused, single-minded, and passive-aggressive character found in Chinese society. I imagine she is unconsciously thinking, "My interest is that I need to get from point A to point B. Yours too. You see me. There are many others like me. This is normal and you are also being careful. We are equal in that, sans pecking order or another society's version of common sense." With child in tow, she is mindlessly careening between cars and buses, betraying her concern or fear. She is merely crossing the street to get to the other side in the most efficient manner available. She is not crazy. She is not afraid. She is not recklessly endangering herself or her child. She is normal. Take that and shove it up your values hierarchy.

The Chinese Reaction

In China, drivers engaged in or affected by the above habits rarely get upset with each other. The police on the roads have other duties and responsibilities and cannot be bothered with these inconsequential violations.

Hence, to answer one of your questions, no, a policeman will not pull over the reckless public bus driver who regularly crosses the double yellow line to give him a ticket. Correcting the above driving habits is not part of their active duty. Traffic law is not strictly enforced by auto patrol and is regarded as significantly less important than other safety concerns.

Chinese streets are constructed with a complete array of traffic cameras including ticket cameras and flicking traffic counter cameras at most every corner and even along the roads.

While in America this is a fiercely debated topic with respect to violation of privacy, here it is simply the primary public safety mechanism all drivers are aware of to keep you from driving too fast.

To the erratic driving, weak enforcement, and scattered pedestrians, we need to add a few other elements to complete the picture of orchestrated yet safe madness.

A working man in a common three-wheeled cargo tricycle is leisurely peddling along on the wrong side of the street. In the back of his cargo tricycle cart is his wife, toddler, and infant child. If you stopped to suggest to them that their cart was in a dangerous place, they would consider you the oddball in the conversation.

Sociology and Confessing to Insanity

I, Mario Cavolo, Italian American, of sound mind, do swear to tell the truth, the whole truth and nothing but the truth.

I am societally brainwashed and because I am brainwashed I behave in ways that are judged highly irresponsible and even criminal in certain other societies on planet Earth.

I further confess I never used to act this way. I also used to be shocked that other people would consistently behave this way.

Then, like a vampire, I became one of them.

I was driving my car along the road back to my apartment. As I turned left into the parking lot entrance gate there were old people on the left and a mother, father, and baby in stroller on the right. Giving them no notice whatsoever I drove past and through them on my left and right. Afterward I realized what I had done, realizing that while I was doing it, I had no conscious judgment of having done so. It had become habit.

It gets worse. The people on the street were also expecting me as the driver to behave that way. They didn't care at all that I did not wait for them to cross the road or politely motion with a wave of my hand for them to go first across the road.

If I had done so, they would have acted confused and wondered what the problem was. "Hey, why is that driver doing something different than we expect, is something wrong?"

I do not hesitate to grant you that every fiber of my being says it is insane to drive your car through the crosswalk while the crosswalk light is green, to weave your car between throngs of people in the crosswalk. If I do not drive this way, the driver behind me will honk their horn wondering why I am not continuing to allow the wheels of my car to spin in the forward direction.

Yet, I do it every time, every day, dozens of times per day as I am expected to in the society in which I live. In fact the traffic light timing encourages such behavior. As a car's left turn arrow is green, so is the pedestrian crosswalk green. And the left arrow turn lanes are on the right side of the road! Whatever those folks down at traffic control are thinking I'll just behave as I'm supposed to.

End confession. Ten Hail Mary's, Father Joe?

We must further ask if the people involved are influenced by any other forces. They are: the law.

The thinking, driven by the legal law with respect to fault and liability, goes like this:

"Hi, Mr. Driver, I know and you know that if your car hits me, it is your fault. That's why I don't care about politeness and manners. I know that you know that hitting me is very bad. In fact, while you are pulling out driving backwards out of your parking space and the reverse lights on your car are lit up, I will still walk with my child or on my bicycle directly behind your car. Because I know that you know that if you hit me, it is still your fault because you didn't look to make absolutely sure no one was sneaking behind you before you allowed your vehicle to move. "

That is the hand-in-hand combination of law and human behavior in China. You are the one behind the wheel of a heavy steel machine on wheels and you are responsible to make sure you don't hit an unprotected person with it no matter what.

Christianity Flourishing and Free in China?

My wife and I attend Sacred Heart Catholic Church in Shanghai, on the west side of the Huangpu River in Pudong.

I'll let that sink in for a moment.

There are several other Catholic and Protestant churches located in Shanghai and all across China's cities welcoming the swelling numbers of Chinese who are joining the Catholic and Protestant churches here as they seek a spiritual root in their lives, their community, and their families.

Another moment. Take your time.

Do feel free to visit the website of the Catholic church we attend.

"What?"

Yes, the web address is www.sacredheartpudong.com.

Relax, go ahead, it's not blocked like Facebook and Twitter.

"Oh, it's not blocked?"

Right, maybe they like the churches in their country more than social media companies! Just kidding.

"Oh, I need a VPN, right?"

No, it's not blocked. None of the Catholic and Protestant Church websites in China are blocked. Just Google "China Catholic Protestant Church locations."

Anyone is free to attend, and every week they do, and more people are joining the Christian religion each year in China than any place else in the world. There's this really cool evangelical-type worship center in Puxi, wow, they really get wild in there, screamin' out "Amens" and "Glory Praise!" and all that.

"Really? Yeah, but . . . "

Wait, I know, I'll get to it. Give me a minute.

And we receive Communion every Sunday, you know, that wafer and wine thing Catholics do.

And I went to confession last month before Mass.

And families arrange baptism for their infants.

This is not the reality you thought you were going to read.

"But what about the house churches they don't allow?"

Yes, I know, please, I'll get to it.

When we attend Mass at Sacred Heart or St. Peters here in Shanghai, there is no difference between the experience we have here compared to the experience we have at St. Maria Goretti Catholic Church back in Scottsdale, Arizona, where my family there has been attending for the past 30 years. Some would say there's exactly the same bad music and boring prayers but that's not where we're going right now.

The Christian churches in Shanghai and all cities across China are well known and publicly free, they typically hold close to 1,000 churchgoers and are packed on Sunday with both Chinese and foreign families. The Mass service is identical to the Mass service performed at any Catholic church across the world. There are masses in English and Mandarin. If I would like, I can go to the sacrament of confession before Mass to be absolved of my sins in the way of the Catholic faith. If a family wishes to arrange a baptism of a newborn, they simply call the church office and arrange to do so.

This is the plain truth. So, then, what is all the fuss about? The only thing we ever read about regarding Christianity in China in Western media is the suppression of underground churches by Communist monsters. The other day I read someone's idiotic tweet whose public Twitter name I am mercifully omitting here that China is trying to eliminate all religion. Good grief, check your sources, please, for the sake of not disseminating bad information and misleading people.

Now we're getting to the point about "house churches," and you are right, they are not officially allowed so let's talk about and explore why. It is because they are not officially registered as are the churches I have spoken of, which everyone can freely attend. So let's ask a better question: "With the churches available publicly, why does anyone need an underground house church in the first place?"

Are you allowed to start your own home "prayer" or "Bible study" group in the United States? Yes, you are.

Now let me ask, are you allowed to start your own "church" that collects non-profit "donations" of any kind?

The answer is that if you want to open your own "official" church like Sacred Heart in Pudong, where money passes hands and your church is part of the community under the laws of the government, you must legally register the existence of that church as a non-profit organization running a particular religion, collecting revenue, keeping records, and acting in compliance with the laws related to city ordinances, revenue donations, and taxes, correct? I am certain that Sacred Heart and St. Peters in Shanghai are registered with the proper authorities in Shanghai as surely as St. Maria Goretti and Our Lady of Perpetual Help are registered with the proper authorities as required in Scottsdale, Arizona.

We might infer that in China the government treats the opening of a church where people are free to pray, sing, and worship more similarly to the opening of a business where people are free to buy and sell goods and services, but you need a license and you need to follow city ordinances and laws. So then, knowing those are the rules where you live, if you instead chose to start your own "underground" church in the United States, you would also be subject to the requirements under the law, yes? If you want to start a public church, you need to find a commercial building and follow the law and pay whatever taxes and fees are due, and if you don't, the authorities will surely show up and shut you down. If you decide to run a prayer group out of your home and you are not a registered business and you are collecting donations, you are breaking the law. If you are also making too much noise with your amazing gospel prayers and praises, that's wonderful, but your neighbors complain because you're not supposed to be running a business or a church group out of your home in that apartment community, so then you will be shut down by the authorities.

I'm talking about the US above, not China, and I don't find anything strange or difficult to understand about this state of affairs in either the US or China. Governments have such rules, which are meant to be followed. You may argue that they should somehow allow even more freedom than they already are and that's a reasonable argument if you wish. But if you are out there in the media space trying to give the world the impression with your asinine tweets that China is hell-bent on suppressing and beating down Christianity in China, I hope you now realize the folly in such, being far from true and accurate.

Now that leaves another matter, the only matter that I find of interest: the Chinese government won't allow the local Catholic church on their sovereign soil inside their country to have the Vatican and Pope be regarded as a direct authority to the Catholic Church in China, bypassing the government in the spirit of complete separation of church and state. Many feel bad about this separation.

They insist on restrictions in this respect but, as I described to you above, they do not stop any individual person in China from practicing the religions of Christianity at known, public, registered Catholic and Protestant churches, which are packed with people every Sunday. Throughout the year the local churches organize typical Catholic "men's" or "women's" or "marriage" retreats that churchgoers may attend.

China is the world's top growth spot for Christianity, but if you want to start a "Bible study" in your home, that's where the matter starts getting dicey and you may not be allowed to do so. There may be no local church nearby, so you wish to have a gathering at your home.

That's understandable. Then your home gathering becomes larger, more regular and formalized, and now it seems like an "underground" church but it's not registered. The local authorities step in when they notice. This state of affairs could be called frustrating but can we say it is happening on the basis of religious repression? I'm not so sure. When there are individual, local cases of such disputes getting out of hand, we all agree that is very unfortunate and wish such things wouldn't happen.

Meanwhile, now you know clear as a bell that Christians in China freely attend their Protestant and Catholic church services; even so, in the eyes of many the situation is less than the ideal arrangement. I am personally grateful that my family and I have the ability living here in China to be able to attend Catholic church and other church and charity event activities such as with Caritas Shanghai, an organization that raises money for needy families and children with special health problems. This is exactly the same as we would do back in the US and I leave the bigger issues to other people to navigate. Meanwhile, this is most likely an unexpectedly positive description of reality on the subject and I hope it supports this important ongoing dialogue.

Patriotism: Sacrifice for Country

Is patriotism and nationalism present in the hearts and minds of most Americans? It certainly is.

The author of *The End of America* and *Give Me Liberty*, and democracy activist Naomi Wolf does a fabulous job of illuminating the deeply held values, beliefs, and responsibilities that define who an "American" truly is. Her in-depth study of America's founders enabled her to recognize the trappings of fading democracy that have crept into the life of the average American citizen in today's world.

The American government certainly hopes citizens will patriotically support its difficult decisions such as military actions against terrorists. However, as Naomi Wolf points out, leaders in America's government also for the most part hope that American citizens will stay out of the political process and let the leaders handle the matters of state. According to her book, a plethora of technical, political, and financial barriers have been erected over the past 20 years to thwart entry into the political arena unless you have millions of dollars. It has become a rich man's world, yet they succeed in making sure that most Americans don't get it and are powerless to do anything about it.

> "And so, my fellow Americans, ask not what your country can do for you; ask what you can do for your country."
>
> President John F. Kennedy

Is it so different in China? No, not really. Chinese citizens have the freedom to pursue their entrepreneurial dreams by starting businesses, to seek a better career, a higher salary, a nicer home. Yet they are mostly unable to influence the decisions of their political leaders. Does that sound vaguely familiar to any American dreamers?

Today's older Chinese parents are experiencing culture shock over what their society has evolved into; they observe their 20-something children living "Chuppie" lifestyles with professional careers at multinational companies earning 5, 10, 20, even 50 times their parents' salaries.

As is the case for American citizens, Chinese citizens are encouraged to support, protect, and serve their country. I would suggest that the single biggest difference between the two in this area is the degree of freedom of speech, but even that distinction isn't the extreme it once was. Though not as free as in the West, Chinese newspapers and magazines more openly publish information on many subjects that were once taboo, including views on homosexuality and critical views on where the current government needs to do more than it is.

Get the Flu, Get Robbed

I went to the hospital with my mother-in-law because I had a fever, having obviously come down with a flu bug of some sort. My mother-in-law and I were in the private exam room waiting.

I was relaxed on the examination table with my latest Baldacci novel and antibiotic IV stuck in the back of my hand. (Chinese doctors routinely prescribe IV treatment rather than pills. It is inexpensive, more effective but less convenient because you have to go to hospital each day and sit there for two hours.)

My mother-in-law left the room for a few minutes. A nicely dressed man walked into the room quickly, looked at me, looked at the medicine being dispensed into my veins as though he was checking it for my benefit, smiled, gave me a thumbs up gesture, headed over to the table behind me, and took a bag that I erroneously assumed belonged to the hospital.

Something about the encounter gave me that "hmm" kind of feeling. Upon her return to the room I asked my mother-in-law whether she had her bag safely with her, more for my peace of mind than in an attempt to reveal a crime. Alas, the thief had absconded with my mother-in-law's purse. I had been duped while feverish.

On another occasion, I walked into a Starbucks in Shanghai's Xujiahui district, placed my winter overcoat on a chair, and proceeded to line up with a few other patrons to place my order.

Only seconds had passed before I turned around to check on my table. My coat was gone. Neighboring customers told me they just saw the thief snatch my coat and run "that way."

Petty thieves such as this roam the halls of hospitals, streets, shopping malls, and neighborhoods all over China looking for an easy grab.

Fortunately, that is typically the worst of Chinese street crime as compared to the United States where the degree of violent crime is much higher. When you consider how much more crowded the cities and streets of China are when compared to the US, it is easy to see how this sort of street crime can flourish.

Frankly, the only other famous global destination where I can personally confirm that such master petty thieves practice their craft is Italy.

Italian pickpockets are masters of their skill. My father had his pocket picked in St. Peter's Square. At Ostia beach outside of Rome, our car was broken into and our bags stolen. Thank heavens I had my passport with me at the time.

Petty Theft - Getting What You Deserve

What typically happens in China when a street thief is caught in the act, for example, of trying to steal a purse, a bicycle, or goods from a vendor?

Let's say that these people are not valued and respected members of society; they are just lowlife, street-level folks trying to survive. The perpetrator gets his due by the neighbors long before the police finally arrive by an ever enlarging circle of the offended and annoyed locals whose stuff he just tried to pilfer.

The seized thief is likely to get a good beating with the males of the neighborhood surrounding him, yelling at him, letting them know exactly what they think of his transgression as the shameful dog that he is. Who would disagree?

They then proceed to kick and beat him for being a lowlife thief. They harass and intimidate and taunt him verbally and physically, generally making him miserable as, indeed, he deserves. After a few minutes the police arrive and start asking questions of the bystanders, but not yet quite intervening in the street entertainment.

Finally, when the police on the scene have decided that enough is enough, they step in and arrest and haul the dismayed and pummeled thief away to the nearest police station to be booked.

Meet a Harvard Trained MD for US$3

A friend in his 50s was having chest pains. He was certain it was a combination of muscular and joint pains as he had recently moved house and had been carrying heavy boxes around. However, wise at age 50, he wanted to be sure so he headed to the Dong Fang #1 Hospital in Pudong. Blood test and EKG revealed no indications that the problem was his heart. Along the way, he was chatting with the doctor who spoke decent English and enjoyed the opportunity to chat in English.

"Ah, you have been to the US? Really? Where?" asked my friend. The doctor replied, "Massachusetts! I studied at Harvard Medical School." Not bad for the three-dollar hospital registration fee.

Two Extremes Moving Toward the Middle

America started as a pure democracy whose ideals, expectations, and laws have shifted more and more toward socialist ideals and policies in most recent years.

Today's American governance is looking more and more like European socialism. The evidence of this is quite easy to find as one follows the path laid out, for example, by the February 2009 cover and article of *Newsweek* entitled "We Are All Socialists Now."

In contrast, one can easily see that China's governance reveals a political system that began at the opposite end of the spectrum with communist/socialist ideals and laws and is progressing toward expansion of individualism. Beginning 30 years ago under Deng Xiaoping, China's governance has shifted drastically toward individual rights, the spirit of capitalist entrepreneurship, and a market economy, yet still transacting trillions on and off the books in cash.

This is not to say that China does not still have many issues that will need to be dealt with in the future. Still, in terms of historical perspective, China has had a remarkable few decades of economic growth and expansion beginning with Deng Xiaoping's opening policies of the '80s, which has resulted in the country becoming an integrated and critical piece in the global market puzzle.

Does it not occur to any pessimist that a massive region of the world is expanding, not contracting, is fueled by trillions in cash and that this statistical fact portends well for the future demand of all "stuff" across the globe? Let me throw in that 50% of the earnings of S&P

500 companies are international, with more and more based in rising Asia. While assuredly not discounting disturbing global financial and economic pressures, pessimists and "permabears" seem to relish discounting the powerful, upward expansionary forces across the global economy that also clearly exist.

The difference in the amounts of cash found in the two societies is easily one of the greatest extremes but we are forced to notice this is not an extreme between the two countries, which are moving toward the middle. We could reasonably surmise that as China continues to modernize, the amount of business transacted in cash and the amount of off-the-books cash will gradually decrease. For example, more and more Chinese are using their debit cards at the grocery store. If they are using their new credit cards because of a points/perks program, 99% of them are paying off the balance each month automatically executed by their bank. No one would be crazy enough to allow a loan balance to accumulate at a 15% or higher interest rate.

In the US, the use of cash is already at a bare minimum across the society with many retailers and service providers simply refusing cash for payments. If they do accept cash, they don't accept anything larger than a $20 and heaven forbid you whip out a $100 bill, a guaranteed way to delay the transaction and meet the manager on duty. American society from the highest levels on down has done everything to steer the spending and business transactions patterns of society away from cash but China is far, far behind on this curve. Perhaps the size of China's cash economy will gradually shrink to half of its current level over the next ten years. It is anybody's guess and will undoubtedly be a subject examined more closely as time goes on.

Lennar Homes NextGen Meets China's "Si Dai Tong Tang"

I have been saying for years that with the societal and economic forces that are in play, as China becomes more Westernized, the US society will become more like China's. In what ways will this happen?

The Asian lifestyle is characterized by savings, frugality, and close, traditional, interdependent family ties.

In other words, you live in the same house with your parents, even after you get married.

And your parents live with their parents, too.

Which means you live with your spouse, your parents, and your grandparents.

In the same house.

And with your children.

Four generations of family living together under one roof. That's what "Si Dai Tong Tang" refers to in Mandarin and we can easily understand that living this way came from the necessity to be frugal, to support and take care of one another on a low budget in a third-world country.

In addition, we also find multiple families sharing the same property together. In the early 2000s when I first moved to Shanghai, I moved into a fabulous 1920s Old Shanghai Lane apartment. The landlord owned all three floors and I rented the studio apartment, which was the back half of the first floor along with a shared kitchen space I didn't use very often. The apartment was decorated in thick, dark mahogany wood with tall, heavy French doors designed with beveled, lead crystal glass and brass accents. It was truly magnificent and rent back then was only $350 per month! My landlord lived with the four generations of their family in the rest of the building on the first, second, and third floors.

Located in the apartment next door, six families shared an identical unit. Two families each living in a room or two on the first floor, the second floor, and the third floor, sharing the bathrooms and kitchens.

Now I can also officially welcome you to the new American neighborhood and multi-generation lifestyle as I read a recent article reporting that Lennar Homes, one of America's best-known homebuilders has designed and is promoting their new concept NextGen home with the first subdivision sold out in Santa Clarita Valley, California. Basically, they take a 3,500-square-foot home and lay it out with additional separate door entrances, bathrooms, and private garden space. Brilliant! What they are in fact doing is also building a house split into one larger and one smaller apartment that you can rent out for rental income.

Don't you worry. I am not saying it will be easy but America will adapt and be just fine. American society possesses a unique, adaptable spirit. As the society transforms, Americans will respond well over time. There is a growing population now well over 100 million in the United States whose lifestyles are becoming tougher and leaner, not more abundant. They will be forced more and more to learn to live together as multiple generations, sharing accommodations with friends or roommates. The next piece of the puzzle will be that out of necessity they will also be working longer hours with two or even three jobs. It looks like Obamacare and related national health care initiatives are going to cause a vast increase in the number of low-wage, part-time workers in the US over the coming years. When you combine these trends together you find the profile of a person who has lost the privacy of their own independent apartment, is sharing with a roommate, but since they are working from 7 a.m. to 8 p.m. six days a week, having their own private space to live is far less important to their well-being.

And yes, here in Shanghai, we are three generations living together; my wife and I, our young son, and his grandma, my mother in law. I wouldn't have it any other way. It is one of the most beautiful and genuine things in this life that we are a happy family together.

The Cash, the Women, the Baby Boom

By now you are hopefully well persuaded in your understanding that the Big Lie is everywhere and that such a way of thinking goes hand in hand with a strong, private, cash economy. In exploring where the money of the cash world is consumed, I will now thread together three ideas starting with some reasonable assumptions along the way—let's see how it all fits together.

We start with an exploration of raw chauvinism and old-fashioned chivalry. Though the divorce rate in China is rapidly rising, it is rising from very low levels. The traditional view of "man pursues woman and woman plays hard to get" relationships along with the traditional marriage/family structure are very much intact. In fact, you can even go to the local city park to find matchmaking families complete with family records trying to find a good match for their heirs. Now that's traditional! Infidelity, China-style, is also commonplace.

By nature some note that ego-driven men like to conquer and build castles. Their castle is empty without their queen, or perhaps a harem. They like money as a means of keeping score, they like to build up collections of spoils to remind them of their success, and in the end, they get the girl, the prize to possess and adore. Just like the Marlboro man riding off on horseback into the sunset with his woman's arms wrapped around his waist. In doing their conquering, historically recalling for example, Helen of Troy, they are often motivated by a woman in the background they are trying to impress, desire, and want to make their queen, or bird in a cage. Considering a stereotypical view of Italian culture, the men place the beauty of women on a pedestal to be admired as the highest form of magnificence and art.

Well, maybe it is not only Italy in which we find such adoration of feminine beauty and the misguided, hormone-driven desire by men to somehow possess it for themselves.

All of which leads me to where a lot of the cash goes in Asia. I do not mean only China. There is a much clearer understanding in China, and also in Japan, that home life may include mutually agreed separation and has a low emphasis on sexual relations, that a husband and even the wife is out playing around for fun as nature calls. In Japan, there are "soap" bars where a man goes to enjoy cavorting with sexy women, yet is devoted to his marriage, to the structure and stability of a home with family and security for which the wife is responsible and respected. In China we witness the endless "barbershop" salons or larger professional health club spas both of which commonly include a "rub 'n' tug" as a healthy way to reduce tension, if not more.

It's indirect, it's understood, and it's in cash. Yes, this type of thinking and behavior is quite prevalent in Asia, and in China it may further develop to a point where a smitten man will arrange his willing "er nai," which means second wife, in an apartment, usually in a second city where he works, where she expects visits accompanied by shopping sprees.

Needless to say, this entire world is a cash world. In a cash world, again we notice it is much easier to keep such matters private and separate, isn't it? Try putting up a lover in an apartment in the US. How will a man pay for the apartment, his American Express? Hollywood movies are filled with such clichés as the spouse unexpectedly discovering a strange credit card purchase at Tiffany's and some Italian bistro. Oops, honey, you weren't supposed to see that.

Regarding the nature of man-woman relationships we now move on to stage two, where a marriage has taken hold, survived, and hits the baby stage in today's urban China. I call it . . .

The Urban Baby Boom Boom Boom

July, 2012

UBM, a global events and exhibitions company.

The Annual China Maternity Baby Exhibition, Shanghai.

The largest ever in the world.

100,000 square meters of exhibitor space.

Record attendance.

A quote as taken from one of my articles at investment advisor Rick Ackerman's website:

> Does it not occur to any pessimist that a massive region of the world is expanding, not contracting, and that this statistical fact portends well for the future demand of all "stuff" across the globe? While assuredly not discounting disturbing global financial and economic pressures, pessimists and permabears seem to relish discounting the powerful, upward expansionary forces across the global economy that also clearly exist.
>
> Here in Shanghai, I now sit in the new upper-middle-class mall called Kerry Parkside. Observing every family that enters this mall, every woman I see is either with a baby/toddler in tow or pregnant. Did I say "every"? Apologies. Of course not, and I readily confess such an exaggeration. Yet it boggles my mind to note how many pregnant women and under-three-year-olds are here, appearing very much as the rule, not the

> exception. The same exact observation is easily made across China's 20 or so major urban centers, now totaling a population well over 300 million family dwellers.
>
> Indeed, the United Nations predicts the addition of 300,000,000 people to China's population in the next generation by 2050 and according to my eyeballs, they are well on their way.

So how did the country once shrouded behind the bamboo curtain become an economic juggernaut?

This examination of reality in China forces me to ask, "How does a country with trillions of cash, cash, cash crash, crash, crash?"

In my estimation this doomsday "crash" eventuality is certainly not a high probability in the grand scheme. The economies of Asia are expanding and that expansion is being led by China with a scope unprecedented in world history. That's the fact, period. Get over it. Understand it. Accept it. Embrace it, because it is very much going to affect everyone's future around the globe including yours.

The domestic growth of China is occurring due to a strength founded in a practical reality that outsiders, especially Americans, on the far side of China's mysterious great wall find difficult to comprehend and easy to ignore.

China today is in many ways in the same position as the US was in 40 years ago. That doesn't mean economic cycles won't give us quite the roller coaster ride over the coming years, but the fundamental core remains. What practical realities are you referring to, one might ask?

In answer to the question, let's look at a selection of key economic and societal indicators that justify a serious reevaluation of the "imminent Chinese doomsday" prognostications. My vote is that they are nonsense; after becoming more informed, what's yours?

Study Abroad

According to recent media reports, "China has the largest number of overseas students in the world, with a record 1.27 million studying abroad at the end of 2010 . . . up 24% over 2009 . . . more than 90% of the students chose to study in the top 10 destinations—the United States, Australia, Japan, the United Kingdom, South Korea, Canada, Singapore, France, Germany, and Russia. Dozens of US colleges and universities are seeing a surge in applications from students in China."

What do these students need in order to study at universities around the globe? Money I believe, and lots of it. Universities across Asia, Europe, and North America are not handing out scholarships begging them to come.

The surge in overseas Chinese students is another perfectly clear indicator of the rise in income and wealth of China's middle and upper class. It is occurring, as many other factors, at an unprecedented rate of growth.

"A recent report from Mintel Group, a London-based market intelligence firm, on Chinese consumer lifestyles reveals that 'despite a life of comfort and privilege, expectations for the Little Emperors are now exceptionally high—as of today, a staggering three quarters (75%) of Chinese middle-class families expect their children to attain a postgraduate degree, a testament to the extent to which higher education is linked with future prosperity in modern China.'"

According to a Mintel 2012 press release, "Two thirds (66%) of middle-class children in the cities attend 'key schools'*, which aim for the majority of their pupils to go on to higher education of some sort."

In these insights, Mintel is referring to what they estimate as a total of over 50 million "Little Emperors" in China, whom I would say are being well groomed for the new global economic playground.

There are other important implications. There seems to be a trend in America along the lines of "a college degree is more and more a waste of time and money." The main supporting reason we hear most often is that even with a college degree it is difficult to find employment.

This is, in my view, dangerously defeatist thinking. If you think it is difficult to get a job with a bachelor's degree, how much harder is it going to be when your incoming competition from Asia for those jobs has an MBA?

In the Driver's Seat

Another practical, leading economic indicator comes from the automobile market. China's auto industry sold 18 million total vehicles in 2010 and 15 million passenger vehicles two years later in 2012.

Recently, we were invited to attend the 14th annual automobile show at the Shanghai New International Exhibition Center in Pudong, next door to our offices at the Kerry Hotel, which included manufacturers, distributors, and suppliers throughout the industry. Imagine over a dozen exhibition halls each the size of a football stadium filled with attendees and you perhaps begin to visualize the enormity of the scene.

The Associated Press reported that GM plans to double auto sales in China. "Some 13.7 million passenger vehicles were sold in the country (China) last year, when sales grew by a third over 2009. GM plans to roll out 60 new and upgraded models in China in the next five years, almost half of them Chevrolets and Buicks . . . "

I'm not praising the glories of flooding the world with a few million more four-wheeled gas guzzlers every year. Yet like it or not, the Chinese automobile market is still in its infancy, a reality that greatly supports related sectors across the entire domestic economy, another practical economic indicator to note.

Give Me a Call Sometime

Next on the list, putting aside for the moment the record-breaking sales of tablet computers, let's consider China's 600 million mobile phone users and 500-plus-million Internet users.

On April 21, 2011, BBC News reported, "China Mobile, the world's largest mobile operator, has surpassed 600 million subscribers after increasing its number of customers in rural areas. The company added 16.8 million users between January and March, it said. China Mobile also said its profits climbed 5.4% to 26.9 billion yuan ($4.1 billion; £2.5 billion) in the quarter, compared with the same period a year earlier."

It's even harder to imagine that with 600 million mobile phone users, there's still another 200 to 300 million to go.

New subscribers are being added at an average rate of 5 million per month according to China Mobile, numbers that make any Western market spasm and drool with envy. With the integration of mobile to the Web 3.0 online experience, the growth in this and related sectors will continue at unprecedented and staggering levels. As reported in a December 2012 *Xinhua* news release, China will add an estimated 100 million new 3G subscribers in 2013, according to the Ministry of Industry and Information Technology (MIIT). The number of broadband Internet users will increase by 25 million.

Blacklisting the World's Largest Retail Economy

We are now going to talk about the world's largest online retail platform: www.taobao.com. Not only is it the world's largest, it is still growing at a staggering rate of 60+% per year. Everyone we know living here in China buys as much stuff as possible on a daily basis online at www.taobao.com—*the* online shopping platform of China—and its retail sister site www.tmall.com

Wonderful, an amazing business success story, right?

Apparently not: Taobao is blacklisted by the US government Trade Office.

> " . . . pirated and counterfeit goods are still widely available on Taobao, the third-most visited website in China."
>
> *Shanghai Daily*

What a fascinating state of affairs.

Tmall.com/Taobao.com is the busiest, biggest online retailer of China, an online retail platform at the nucleus of China's expanding domestic retail economy, one of the most scrutinized, leading economic indicators across the world today.

If you can believe this, each year, 11/11 (November 11) is the traditional "sale" day on Tmall and a staggering 230 million registered users were online on that single day while 106 million of them made a purchase. To clarify how these online shopping sites work relative to similar platforms in the West, you may regard Tmall as the commercial-level platform similar to Amazon, while Taobao is like eBay, an individual-level platform.

Yet at the same time, we note it is found on the US Trade Office notorious marketers' blacklist.

Now bear with me here. I believe I know what you are thinking right now: "Oh, yeah, China; all that fake, cheap stuff."

Yes, that is in many ways true, but if I had just instead reported to you that " . . . the core retail domestic economy of the entire continent of Europe is on the US trade office blacklist," you would have probably stopped with a big "Whoa!" sensing much larger implications in such a state of affairs, which is why we are discussing it here.

Our focus right here and now is not on whether or not China is a purveyor of cheap, fake goods. Our focus is on the rather astonishing paradox that in essence, the core domestic retail economy of what is in a few short years going to be the world's single largest GDP economy is now blacklisted by the US government Trade Office.

What does this mean in the grander scale? It demands a closer look including what it means for the global economy, not to mention US–Sino relations. So, let's take a closer look not by expected business analysis but by another more personal story; looking at the adventures of a typical mom in China who needs to buy baby formula for her infant.

The first point to make is that no matter what brand she purchases, many mothers will buy it online through Tmall/Taobao.com, whose online shops often also have a retail shop somewhere and will deliver to your home the next day. (Delivery of goods all over China is really cheap. It might cost $5 to have a typical 3–4 day parcel sent from Guangzhou to Shanghai.) But in the explosion of online retail, the virtues of cost-savings and cheap home delivery are the least important part of this story.

Ninety percent of this story is about fear. Ninety percent of a Chinese mom's time and effort in this otherwise common, daily consumer purchase is spent insuring that what she is buying is not either a fake copy or an illegal import. In this first case, a fake copy, mom's concern is deepest. How much of your time and energy while shopping online in America is spent doing that?

For example, even in China's large supermarkets, as I purchase my personal Italian kitchen essential, extra virgin olive oil, I may find two bottles of the exact same brand with the label looking "almost" the same.

Remembering the warning of my first true Chinese friend Frank from Chongqing,

"Mario, assume everything is fake; we do."

I was simply unable to confirm what the hell I was buying. Asking the store supervisor is a waste of time as of course you are going to get no good answer from them beyond saying that the supplier sent them that way, when in fact, one of the managers may have made a side deal with a bootleg distributor to make some extra money. Now we're putting our finger on one of the downsides of the off-the-books cash economy: loss of control not in terms of the government collecting taxes or insuring businesses are licensed, but in terms of controlling the quality of the supply chain.

Facing these issues as a consumer is the daily rule, not the exception, though let's acknowledge that the tide of transparency in business is improving and turning for the better over time. A Chinese consumer's set of rules to follow might look something like this:

> Rule #1. Completely ignore all Chinese-brand baby formula. To be fair, there are dozens of good quality brands used by hundreds of millions of families all across the country. Yes, as the Chinese newspapers regularly report, quality control issues are a ubiquitous problem, and so to be safe, skip them completely.
>
> Rule #2. Take every opportunity possible when you have a friend going across the border to another country to please bring back a few boxes of a foreign brand. Failing in that effort and not to mention how inconvenient it is . . .

Rule #3. Find and choose an imported baby formula brand such as Nutrilon from Holland. Great.

Rule #4. Determine if a particular online shop offers real Nutrilon or fake Nutrilon.

There it is. Whether being purchased online or in a retail market, that puts us right back to the grave concern about whether what I am holding in my hand is the real thing. The box can easily be copied and faked. The industry in China is expert at it. There are different types of box packaging. Huh? Some boxes are exactly as they appear on the brand's international website.

Other boxes are genuine, by legal license, and designed in the local market where the baby powder is imported in bulk and then packaged locally. Reasonable, except one is fake, one is not; one is illegal, one is not.

There is a small white "import" sticker with details on all such imported products. That can easily also be faked and everyone knows it. Companies put special labels and codes and stamps on their boxes to make it very difficult for counterfeiters to duplicate, in the same way a country uses such strategies to avoid counterfeit of their currency.

The actual baby formula powder inside the container is also almost impossible to be sure of. Again, this may be imported by authorized reseller and packaged locally. But a pirate distributor may use local baby formula and simply package it into fake boxes they have copied.

The evolution of the story remains as a simmering stew, slowly changing, yet essentially the same. For the Chinese consumer it's to face a daily, big, fat caveat emptor, which they regard as a given. "Yeah, of course, we know, we deal with it," they say.

When buying a Chinese brand of olive oil, you are buying olive oil that has been imported in bulk and then bottled and labeled in China. When you buy a bottle of a well-known brand Italian olive oil, you are buying the individual bottle that has been imported and has information written in Italian, ditto for any imported wine or any other product that is obviously imported from its country of origin. When buying a brand of French wine where the sticker is written in Chinese, you are buying French wine that has been imported in bulk and then bottled and labeled in China for distribution.

Pretty much no matter what you are buying, from big furniture to baby formula to office supplies to a new faucet for your bathroom sink, you can buy it on Taobao and have it delivered.

For the US Trade Office blacklist, it's putting them on notice, taking a stand for good reason, forcing China's regulatory and supply chain structure to improve, which it is, and so serving the public good in terms of product safety and quality.

Now, let's take a look at my favorite indicator of the state of the domestic economy, which few others seem to value highly enough.

More on Mortgage Free

China's lower and middle-class strata presently reside in 100–150 million mortgage-free homes. Let's set some parameters and take a look:

1. Many families' apartments in China are small at around 40 square meters or less (400 square feet), many are around 80 square meters with 2 or 3 bedrooms, and there are also many apartments in the 100- to 130-square-meter, 3- to 4-bedroom range.

2. Home values across the broad urban market are now at RMB 5,000 to 8,000 per square meter ($80–$135 per square foot.)

3. Therefore, we have a typical 80-square-meter, 2-bedroom apartment now worth an average of RMB 400,000–640,000 ($70,000–$108,000)

Adding up the average numbers leads us to a median average estimated US$15 trillion of mortgage-free home equity. That clearly means that should prices go into a more serious decline, homeowners will still not feel the pressure from being upside down in their mortgage as happened in the US in step with the 2008 financial crisis and subprime debacle. Furthermore, of those homes that do have a mortgage, the average down payment was not 5–10% but 30% or higher, so again, far less debt leverage exists in China.

It is critical to note that the sector of urban home ownership I am focusing on here does *not* include the bubble-stretching, high-priced, luxury property market that exists in China's first-tier cities (Shanghai, Beijing, Shenzhen, Guangzhou) which total only 10% of the aggregate real estate market in China.

If the Chinese middle-class homeowner masses, in cahoots with the growing encouragement of the major banking industry brands, started borrowing on those homes, even at only 20% of equity, that would put an additional US$3 *trillion* into the state of rising domestic spending.

Even with an economic slowdown there is no reason to believe that this property sector will drop in value more than 10% from current levels, or even at all. Most recently as we start moving through 2012–13, indications are there that the property market softened, with over-leveraged property developers cutting prices to encourage buyers, followed by a trend of prices firming and rising again as we head into 2014.

I continue to suggest that situations of strong price appreciation are isolated, not representative of the broad domestic market where most buyers have already bought, enjoying the permanent benefits of substantial yet reasonable appreciation on the value of their properties. If we want to talk about prices of homes across America, we're not going to talk about nosebleed prices just in Manhattan or Newport Beach or Seattle, we are going to look more broadly at many other American mainstream cities where home prices are far lower. The same reasonable analysis applies in China with prime areas supporting nosebleed property prices for the upper class while more broadly across China's mainstream cities prices are far more reasonable. In fact, mainstream, broad, residential property prices in China are very similar to home prices across the US, and by now you realize, there is a middle class that can afford them far more easily than previously understood.

1. If you still don't quite get it, realize that an average home in the United States in the 1960–70s was available for purchase in the $25,000 to $50,000 range. Those homes today, even after the recent real estate crash, are valued at $90,000 to $200,000. I am hard-pressed to suggest they will go down further in value from today's prices. Ditto in China.

2. Economic analysis of China almost always discounts the $6-10 *trillion* off-the-books cash economy. The cash-only grey economy has massive economic power and security completely separate

from any officially reported GDP or other open economic statistics available on China. The only fairly reliable study and report on this subject was released in 2010 by Credit Suisse and worth researching.

3. Lamentations over China's few ghost towns and empty apartments are utter nonsense precisely because there are, relatively speaking, just a few of them. This is easy to understand. In a country of 1.3 billion people with 200 million more people continually migrating to the urban areas and who need a place to live, who cares about a dozen or so failed small city real estate expansions?

To be fair, the local folks who were caught up in such projects and sustained losses are the losers, and our empathy rightfully goes out to them. Yet, the point here is that such stories and situations are an exception, plainly not a broad representation of the real estate market as a whole.

China is the most rapidly urbanizing country in the world, with millions of people moving from the countryside into the city—an urban migration unprecedented and a socioeconomic trend that shows no signs of abating for years to come. Keeping that context in mind, one also needs to understand that holding empty apartments is a common choice for asset store in China, just like a bar of gold or stock. I need to repeat this point; in America people do not regard a home as a store of value such as a bar of gold, while here in China they do.

It is common for apartments to be bought as a concrete shell and held as speculative investments while the surrounding area is still under development. Hence, for one to three years, apartments are empty. Here in China, this is normal and no one is concerned about it. The property is just an asset holding, sitting there like a bar of gold.

This marketplace is certainly not perfect. Real estate development failures do exist; excess supply is not a bizarre and rare occurrence. There is a buildup of inventory that needs time to be absorbed but to dwell on China's ghost town phenomenon as representative of what is happening in the broad society of home property ownership is deeply misguided.

There are a whopping total of seven ghost towns, small communities in a country expected to have over 200 cities with a population over one million in the next ten years. Doesn't seem like the weighty economic indicator that some purport it to be, does it?

The last place anyone on planet earth should be expecting an economic crisis is in the rise of Asia led by China, or perhaps Lichtenstein. (That was a joke.) Lots of debt, lots of building surely, but matched by lots of cash and lots of growth.

Evaluate the practical reality and consider the motivation behind the media stories you come across on China—is there reasoned analysis or do the arguments depend too highly on classic negative rhetoric?

Saving $200 per Month on a $600 per Month Salary?

China had endured and struggled through the past 30 years as the country exited Mao's Cultural Revolution. From those challenging experiences, many Chinese people developed a mindset of self-sufficiency—not expecting meaningful government support, not being able to turn to any meaningful government retirement or welfare-type program such as the US's Social Security, not relying on anything besides their own determination to make a living and save to survive the future. On their own, they learned to share and save to support one another in the local environment, spawning the unmistakable characteristics of their merchant economy.

And so, they have figured out through simple survival instinct, how not to waste a single penny of their hard-earned wages. In this circumstance, they had to think more entrepreneurially, negotiate more, and for too many, learn to gain by cheating, without scruples, without the ethical need for win-win.

For example, even to this modern day, many Chinese with plenty of money in the bank will not use the heat in the wintertime. Why waste the money when all one needs is thicker clothing, just like scientific researchers in Antarctica? They will not turn on a light; they will leave the public hallways dark because they don't want to pay for lighting public space that doesn't belong to them.

Restaurants you love to frequent are freezing cold in the winter because the owner told the staff not to turn on the heat to save money. Sit down, eat, enjoy! Just leave your coat on. What's wrong with that?

Restaurant customers across China know this and expect they will continue to wear their coats after sitting down to dine and the restaurant is still busy. As the sociologist in me often observes, normal behavior is normal, people don't consider it as a factor in their decision when that same behavior or circumstance is all around them.

After lunch and before dinnertime, even the lights in the restaurant are turned off to save money. In America, "standards," whatever the hell that means, are expected to be maintained for customers even at mid-level establishments. And if they are not, someone fills out a complaint card or asks for compensation for being inconvenienced! It's a different world. That's much more important than not wasting money on electricity for lighting and heating.

So let's realize there is no objective right/wrong or should/shouldn't. It is only a matter of what value system hierarchy exists within your particular culture and society.

But Wait—A 50% Savings Rate?

According a November 2012 article by CCTV reporter Han Peng, recent IMF figures show China's personal savings rate has surpassed all other countries in the world, with an average rate of over 50%. The world's average savings rate is no more than 20%.

Wait a sec, that sounds preposterous and I'm taking a closer look.

We can start by easily agreeing with the following article quote from Zhao Longkai, economist of Peking University, who said, "The fundamental reason for such high savings is uncertainty about future. Without an adequate social welfare system, many people have to save enough money on their own for their pension and medical expenses. That's especially true for the middle-aged generation, who would otherwise be a major force of consumption. Not only do they have to save money for their elderly parents, they are also worrying about their children's education and healthcare."

Those points taken together do make perfect sense. However, now we part ways as I ask, "In an expanding country with high inflation where in the past three years the price of nearly every staple from pork and chicken to garlic, ginger, and car washes has doubled if not tripled, and at the same time with average annual salaries of RMB 3,000 (US$500), the savings rate is up to *fifty percent*, not down? Even as I have illustrated and praised the many pleasures of low-cost living in China, how could the "average person's monthly budget expenses come to only RMB 1,500? (That's half of a RMB 3,000 salary.)"

The first problem is inaccuracy from an error called generalization. People including writers are guilty of mixing precise information with generalities to make an idea seem plausible. As I look at the words in the article, I read the "average salary" and I immediately am taught to ask *who's* average salary? What percentage of the population at *that* average salary? If half earn a RMB 1,000 salary and the other half earn a RMB 5,000 salary, that's an average of RMB 3,000.

Now I will agree that some but not most Chinese earning RMB 5,000 per month are able to save 50% because they live at home or rent a cheap room in an apartment and eat cheap street food and when they are not working they are home reading a book and that's their life and that's truly all there is to the simple story.

For all the rest of the people in this story as is publicly reported to us who earn RMB 3,000 per month and save half of it, I say that's utter bullshit.

The "Big Lie" is what is going on unsaid and unreported; the natural eagerness and attention of a person on a low salary always seeking to make some additional money part time, which as I have explained would most likely be in cash.

Meanwhile, let's ask; how do the Chinese think about money?

Obsessed with Money

Scene 1: Jacuzzi Chitchat

My wife and I were sitting in the jacuzzi at Narada Hot Springs Resort located 90 minutes north of Sanya in the lush mountain rainforests of tropical tourist destination Hainan Island. The two middle-aged ladies opposite us were Shanghainese. We knew this from their demeanor and dialect, the same way one would spot a New Yorker or a Texan in America.

Within no more than five minutes of standard, polite chitchat they proceeded to ask questions in a conversation that went something like this:

"Oh, how nice to be here at this lovely resort. How much did you pay for your room? Which kind of room are you staying in? Did you get a discount or . . . ?"

"Ah, you are staying in a standard room? Ahh, ahh, *we* are in a suite, in one of the villas up on the higher part of the hillside. We paid $300 pert night and it's so lovely."

Scene 2: Taxicab Encounters

This title may lead you to think that I was about to offer a few useful Chinese phrases to employ while in a taxi. No, no; this little essay is about the classic conversation a foreigner will have with a taxi driver in Shanghai.

These are the ubiquitous questions posed to the foreign passenger, almost without fail, day in and day out. Let me remind you that taxi fares are comparatively cheap in China and so the hiring of a cab is a typical expense in the daily lifestyle of the mid-level-and-above wage earner. It is not uncommon for the majority who do not own a car to "grab a cab" three or four times a day.

"What country are you from? Are you American or European?"

"How long are you staying here? What do you do here? Just visiting? Do you work here?"

"Do you like China? How does it compare to your country? Style? Expenses? Weather?"

"Did you buy a house here? How much did you pay for it? Do you rent? How much do you pay for rent each month?"

"How much money do you earn each month?"

"Do you own a car? What kind? Did you get a loan?"

These open queries into the uncomfortable secrets of your life are asked freely to compare how you are doing in the Big Lie. A conversation which would be completely off limits in one culture is common fodder for chitchat in another, such as China.

We can also note a less gossipy side to these examples; these conversations simply have a higher degree of natural human curiosity at their core. This is easy to understand as we realize that Chinese society has just recently reached a time of brand-new opening up and expanding, exposing it to new circumstances and behaviors the Chinese have never experienced before.

It is truly hard to understand that just a few years earlier, there was no such thing as leisure shopping at the mall and certainly not a five-star mountain resort for them to go to on holiday! I am a naturally curious person, the type who likes to ask a million pain-in-the-ass questions when I encounter something new. I think many readers can relate to that kind of natural human curiosity, which is often found in the daily life of the new China.

If You Haven't Tasted a Mango . . .

. . . then you can't explain to anyone else what you think it might taste like. When we are talking about the general economic and business environment with respect to China, I wish to cut through the ridiculous political and cultural misconceptions that bias most of what's written about China by supposed experts and analysts who don't even live here or falsely believe that visiting here several times per year is "good enough."

That bias misleads you and can cost you. As a foreigner living outside of China, you already have the tremendous disadvantage of unavoidable misunderstandings when it comes to understanding most every aspect of Chinese business, politics, and culture.

For example, how can you, living in the United States, explain, accept, and justify watching a woman with her two children mindlessly, calmly, slowly walking across the street through the most chaotic traffic you have ever seen complete with public buses that swerve in and out of their lanes, run red lights, and turn left when they shouldn't even more than the cars do?

Such behavior is incomprehensible to you. In fact, it is borderline criminal and can easily result in your children being taken from your legal custody and placed in a foster home while you enter the mad, mad word of the American family court system.

However, such behavior is neither strange nor criminal here in China. If you walked up to that woman as she reached the other side of the street chiding her for endangering her own life and the lives of her children, she would look at you like you were the one who belonged in an institution.

What, you ask, does that have to do with the price of the Shanghai stock index? Well, it's a point not about the woman, but about the cultural consciousness in China; that woman could easily be the VP of marketing or strategic M&A for Lenovo or Bank of China. She makes important business decisions affecting the company, its competitors, its customers, and ultimately its stock. Don't you think you might like to know how she thinks on a daily basis? How her value system works? How she views *risk* in different contexts?

The Chinese consider things "in context," not in absolutes. Let those words burn into your consciousness. How could you otherwise hope to successfully negotiate business with her or understand how a company in China is run by its owners and managers? I am leading to the point that there is a "cultural consciousness" and "doing business consciousness" you simply can't comprehend. I want to help you close that gap.

Holding Your Tongue

The foreign business people I know here in China who will most discourage a foreigner to attempt to negotiate serious business in Chinese are the ones who are most fluent in the language!

It's a classic and instructive case of "the more you know, the more you realize how little you know." They will warn you to use a formal, trained interpreter, to use a lawyer. Don't bother with your Chinese when it gets down to the brass tacks of the deal. The more fluent they became, the more they understood the culture, the thinking, and the more they knew they were guppies in a shark tank.

Millions of business people in China, like the lady in the above example, operate by a completely different set of values and beliefs and attitudes and rules in thinking about such personal and business choices on a day-to-day basis.

They *think* completely different than you. If you can't think like a Chinese, you can't understand China or anything about China. And in this thinking process, the link between culture and business is inexorably and unalterably fused.

Distortions and Sipping Green Tea

Distortions regarding most every aspect of Chinese business and Chinese culture are a global disease. It infuriates me and it is my mission to constantly correct it with respect to each key influential perspective you must understand.

To what degree am I qualified to accomplish this feat? I know what it means to "think and act like a Chinese." My social and business circle of foreigners have also lived here at least 10 years, most of them happily married with a Chinese wife, same as myself.

I mention this because yes, it does matter. We will never "be" Chinese, but as much as realistically possible, we have earned the nickname with which Chinese refer to us: An Old China Hand. We speak the language. We discuss business in Chinese. (My own Chinese language skills are quite good, but I dare not say fluent!) We understand most of the subtleties in the language base. I can have a healthy argument with my wife, in Chinese!

So, to you then, my Chinese is pretty amazing. If I have to give a longer speech or emcee an event in Chinese, for example, I have to be given that language well in advance and study several extra hours to be able to deliver that particular vocabulary.

I once played a supporting role to famous Hong Kong and Chinese actors in a Beijing CCTV national TV mini-series entitled "Crazy Dancing Lady." I had over 700 lines in 40 scenes during the course of the shooting. I spent 18-hour days on the set, learning my lines while having to communicate with the director and the crew and with famous actors and actresses like Zhen Zhe Wei (Eric Tsang), China's #1 male supermodel, Hu Bing, and Cecilia Yip. *That's* how I learned my Chinese, in the real world, with all of the subtle meaning and emotions attached.

We understand and have internalized the completely different set of values and context in relationships, business discussions, negotiating style, and strategy. We know that in China, communication of direct meaning is rare. A "no" is rare. Hiding relevant information on the other hand, is common.

The attitude is "Why should I reveal my advantage if you don't know about it?" Americans regard that as deceit. Chinese can't understand why you would be so stupid as to show your hand. But it depends, on the "situation," the "context."

We understand the macro and micro business environment of China. I have my consensus set of resources hand picked and filtered over the years. I can smell a moron a mile away.

Those of us in China for over 10 years can typically tell within less than a minute of watching another foreigner whether or not he or she is a new arrival, less than two years, or an old hand. We're swimming in the Chinese business and culture vibe every minute of the day right here on the ground in China—in business and cultural attitudes, mindset, and context.

Here's an example from the investment world: well-known investor Jim Chanos's recent commentary calling for a property bubble in China. I read the context within which such statements are made and quickly get annoyed when I know darn well that such comments are being made out of proper context.

They are far too rhetorical and don't add up in reality to what is really going on here in China. I don't know Jim Chanos and I'm not really trying to knock the guy. I just know that anyone who is here in China in the thick of it right now knows that talk about a bubble in that intended context of the word "bubbles" is just plain silly. The guy doesn't even live here.

I have lived in China for 13 years. I am on the ground; my finger is on the pulse. By the way, I am not saying a bubble couldn't or wouldn't burst. I am saying those comments are as broad and general as to make them meaningless headlines.

Let's look from another angle at the property market in China. If property prices in China's 10 major cities go down 30% from current levels, so what? You think that's a problem or a bursting bubble? Oh, please! 50% of the property owners don't even have mortgages! The other 50% paid an average of a 30% down payment for their mortgages and those mortgages are mostly 10 to 20 years because Chinese are not dumb enough to get a 30-year mortgage where the bank rapes you on interest charges during the first 10 years.

Chinese *don't care*. They bought the apartment; they will pass it on to their children or sell it five years later. We're talking about hundreds of millions of homes that fall into this circumstance I am describing. Such a supposed 30% bubble crash doomsday scenario would be no more annoying than a buzzing mosquito interrupting a sip of green tea.

Chinese RMB Bank Account: You Mean You Don't Have One Yet?

For those millions of us who are living overseas in China, it makes sense that our money in a Chinese bank would be in RMB, the local currency. But in today's world, we all need to think like global citizens and consider the mix of currencies our assets are valued in no matter what country we happen to live in.

You want at least some of your money in a strong currency, right? Then why isn't some of your cash money allocated in Chinese RMB?

If it is possible for you to have some of your money in Chinese RMB or Hong Kong or Singapore currency, do it. So, then, how easy is it to open a bank account? It requires a few simple steps to open one; for example, with HSBC in Hong Kong, it requires making a wire transfer deposit and then converting your USD into another currency. That's it. In fact, HSBC has highly integrated service where all of your accounts all over the world are linked and easily accessed across their platform.

Let me note this is a 100% reasonable, transparent, and legal thing to do with your money that has nothing to do with trying to hide money offshore from your government tax authorities. Your money is yours.

For example, if you went on holiday in Brazil and while there, you decided to open a bank account and deposit $8,000, which would earn 6% sitting in your Brazil bank account, America's Uncle Sam couldn't care less. You're free to do that and it is just another item to include as your listed assets when you do your tax return.

Many people regularly travel to the same destination each year and so they open a bank account locally at that destination. Canadians who spend the winter months living in Scottsdale, Arizona, stop in at the Motor Vehicle Bureau, get a state ID, and are then free to open a local bank or even stock brokerage account in the United States.

Ditto for people who travel each year to enjoy the tropical weather and culture of Thailand. It is simple to open a local bank account and leave some money there at your fingertips when you arrive.

In the major Chinese banks such as Bank of China or ICBC, bank accounts are multi-currency, which is very convenient. You can easily convert foreign exchange online and you can even instantly buy and sell gold and silver.

Do you think I should convert my RMB to USD or Euros or Hong Kong dollars or Japanese yen? Of course not! I know the Chinese banks have done a lot of lending, but its lending level is more than matched by its *cash, cash, cash.*

The RMB is pegged artificially low against the USD and I highly doubt the Chinese government is going to do anything about that any time soon other than allow it to slowly appreciate, which they are.

He who has the cash is king and right now the only country with the cash is China.

I believe it was Pulitzer Prize–winning columnist and author Thomas Friedman who quipped that shorting a country with a trillion dollars cash is a bad idea.

When we say Greater China, we include Mainland China, Hong Kong, Macau, Taiwan. Feel free to add in another cash-rich country and excellent place to park your money: Singapore.

Its Business, Not Politics

Regarding China's overall policies on business, government ideals, and their strong belief that more strict censorship is better for the harmony of the country and government, they remain strongly and stubbornly on that path of doing things their way.

One could applaud Google a while back for taking the moral high ground, for making a statement to the world of what they believe in. Good for them. However, if they did so thinking there was any hope the Chinese might change their policy or business guidelines, they were in a delusional fantasy. National interest plus self-interest defines their priorities and I don't know that it is much different with any other country.

In addition, let me put forth a rather obvious state of affairs business-wise. China blocks websites like Google, YouTube, Twitter, and Facebook, not to censor, but more to allow their own home-grown version of those businesses such as Baidu, Kaixin, Weibo, and WeChat to prosper.

It's just business folks; think about it.

The Sheer Absurdity that China Has a Real Estate Bubble Ready to Collapse

I am certainly not mincing words here with my position on this subject so let's see if we have a rigorous enough viewpoint to support it.

Case 1. Purchase a typical suburban US home in the 1970s.

Cost: $30,000–$50,000

Value in 2012: $130,000–$200,000 (that's post 2008 crash values).

Case 2. Purchase a typical suburban Chinese apartment in the late 1990s.

Cost: $30,000–$50,000 (yes, approximately the same as in the US 30 to 40 years earlier).

Value in 2012: $100,000–$200,000

So, please tell me, what's the big deal? Apparently, it is not true that enough Chinese can't afford to buy homes, supporting relatively reasonable real estate prices when you look at the trend of real estate prices in other markets such as the US where today's real estate is regarded as a bargain compared to prices in Europe, Australia, and Canada. Several additional underlying factors are integral to supporting the notion:

The values of the typical middle-class home for both countries today are in the exact same range. I am speaking of the broad, suburban, lower- and middle-class housing market, not the prime location, first-tier city markets commonly found in the headlines.

Second, the only difference in terms of value appreciation is the length of time from the starting date. Due to factors well known in societal and technological development all across the world, the rate of change in our lifetimes has been increasing. This is well reflected and documented in China's rapid expansion since the 1990s, a cycle of urban, industrial and commercial expansion that took four times longer (four decades compared to one decade) in the United States sans today's technological, industrial, Internet, and wireless-based capabilities.

Third, you may say to me that relative even to those current housing prices, the average income-to-housing-cost ratio is still far too high.

After learning about the "Big Lie" and other points in this narrative, I can only hope by now you would understand that is not the case for many people for whom on the surface this seems to be the case!

Fourth, as was the case in the United States property market, there is no compelling pressure for property owners to sell if prices do decline when they don't have a mortgage or have a smaller mortgage.

Fifth, at the current price levels I have pegged, owners are enjoying appreciation of two to four times the price they paid for their home on which they have no mortgage. How would (or did) you feel if you were in the right place at the right time; if you had bought a home for $50,000 cash and five years later it was worth $150,000–$200,000 with a high likelihood prices are not ever going to go back below that current level? That's a pretty sweet state of affairs, isn't it?

Ninety Percent Home Ownership

There are tens of millions of average Chinese families who all own their own apartment home with no mortgage. They originally paid as little as $15 to $30 per square foot for their homes only ten short years earlier.

Across many cities across the country, those properties are now worth no less than triple that, and in China's dozen or so primary cities, they are worth 5 to 10 times higher. Now let's ask: How many people and how many homes are we actually talking about?

According to the first comprehensive report of its kind released in 2012 by Tsinghua University, 90% of Chinese families own their homes.

My best guess is well over 100 million families, which would be almost half the population of the United States, became much, much wealthier than they ever were before and with zero credit card, mortgage, or car payment debt to bog them down financially.

Notice I am not addressing the upper-middle-income and wealthy, upper-income sectors here. Our observations here are focused on the low- to lower-middle-income sector of people who have had modest lives but always owned a home because that is a foundational part of Chinese culture. Of course such trends are shifting but for those hundreds of millions who were homeowners, it is truly their day in the sun.

On the province of Hainan Island, the local people are Hainan local Li ethnic minority. They are mostly uneducated farmers and fishermen who do not even speak Mandarin, only the local dialect. Their typical apartment has increased in value from the $20,000 they paid for it to $150,000. Many of these folks owned multiple apartments. In using the province of Hainan Island as a representative example of the provinces all across China, the misunderstanding on this point in the rest of the world is astounding.

I am much more concerned that in the coming months and years, there will be more and more indications that China "tells the US to take a hike," as investment advisor Rick Ackerman recently put it in one of his market commentaries. I am very confused as to how so many high officials, gurus, and politicians seem to not know which side the global bread is buttered on. It is buttered, my friends, on the *cash, cash, cash side plus huge property equity* side.

During the past year, foreign businesses in China have experienced deteriorating, not improving levels of difficulty and inconvenience to do business. With the asset and property values rising and enough economic growth humming along, the Chinese are not acting humble and make no mistake, they have no warm and fuzzy plans to become a multicultural, international society.

America wants everything done the American way, am I right or wrong on that? America takes whatever cultural interest exists externally and Americanize them inside American society. The Chinese attitude and plan for the future of their society is no different.

What Do You Admire Most About Chinese People?

It is easy to be a critic. Is it just as easy to find reasons to praise? The question, "What do you admire most about Chinese people?" was recently asked by another veteran expat friend. As my mind immediately began churning through the list of possible answers, it also reminded me of the classic list of complaints foreigners typically say about Chinese people, so let's start there

Chinese are not friendly. Well, they are very friendly amongst their own friends but not particularly friendly with a lack of trust toward strangers. The reasons for this type of behavior should be clear to you by now. We've talked about how they typically form smaller groups of trusted friends and also how they don't show physical affection to one another in public compared to the more double-face-kiss type of Europeans and back-slapping, bear hugging Americans. Instead, Chinese typically offer a gesture to show their caring.

Chinese are childish and selfish. I feel the need to redefine this as "narrow-minded, self-interested, single-minded, focused." Yes, they often come across as childish yet redefining that quality also identifies how it is they successfully navigate and achieve their wants and needs. In contrast, a bias would describe Americans as know-it-alls and annoyingly demanding. Well, this is also "true" yet it also has its dual nature. Americans truly do know a lot more about a lot of things than a Chinese. If you don't believe me, put a typical 18-year-old American teenager up against a typical 18-year-old Chinese teenager and you will quickly understand.

With those criticisms in mind, let's now focus on "What do you admire most about Chinese people?"

They get things done fast. Who can complain about how supposedly lazy they are when they are also capable of building infrastructure across an entire county five times faster than the amount of time it takes in the West?

They are loyal and protective of one another. The closest Chinese business partners we have happen to be Shanghainese. They are as genuine and caring and honest as you could hope any friend or business partner to be, becoming like family. We have never had an argument over one single dollar during our business dealings over a decade of dealings. When I wanted to marry my wife, her best friend wanted to speak to me, to interview me, to ask me very important questions about my intentions, like a protective older sister. Bravo, I think that's terrific.

Chinese are disciplined and diligent. Chalk up this part of their character to the education system. Once again, a double-edged sword where the Asians who kick ass in mathematics and get top grades at foreign universities also lack the skills to be assertive, express their opinions, creativity, and assertiveness.

China's Tropical Paradise

When the government recently announced for the umpteenth time that Hainan Island was going to become an international island, it was no more than a smart PR campaign.

Furthermore, at the very first Boao International Tourism Forum this month, the event was, as expected, very Chinese and very focused on making Hainan an "elite" island destination for the super rich—that's the Chinese super rich, not super rich anyone else.

On this point, I am amazed to see this scary yet obvious parallel between two very different societies. We can observe what's happening in the fabric of the United States and quite easily come to the conclusion that the elitist rich have taken over. The government has less and less to do with "of the people, by the people, for the people." China, as a country compared to the United States, is a very different breed of cat, yet in regard to the wealthy, I am witnessing the exact same game playing out thse past two years; it's all about the super rich.

We make our final and crucial distinction: because the two countries are at different ends of the economic expansion and growth cycles, the elitist super-rich agenda in China is trickling down into the middle-class and lower-middle-class property market values enriching the middle-class, while in America, it is quite the opposite, whereby the super rich have taken over at the expense of the middle-class American dream.

I am now going to dig deep into some information on Hainan Island because this is the primary domestic tropical place where the new middle class and the upper class will take their holidays. To cater to this luxury class there is an unprecedented boom in development.

Though there may have been a global recession, this, of all places on Earth, may have felt that recession least. You certainly would not see recession in the new housing development or in the number of sport and luxury brand automobiles cruising along the streets and the shopping or dining across the island in luxury establishments.

Domestic Vacations

We also need to understand Chinese culture and mentality. They like their way. They don't want to integrate as much as people in the West do. Just look at the Chinese community of 1,000,000 plus in Los Angeles.

They are primarily concentrated in the El Monte area and keep to themselves inside their own community culture. Of course they would travel internationally if they could afford it. But even then it's not that convenient compared to staying within your own country.

Consider how many Americans, only 20% of whom even have passports, do exactly that. They stay in America, which in fact is part of a land mass offering magnificent travel and holiday destinations to enjoy. Most Americans will stay in their own country on holiday. Ditto for the Chinese mainlanders.

Hainan Housing Supply

Let's say that along the 200-kilometer southern and eastern coastline of Sanya, an additional 200,000 apartments are built. That's an enormous number. But relative to what-sized market of potential buyers?

Mainland China's millionaires number in the millions, plus she has a rising middle-class population the size of the United States' entire population with low household debt levels, and they basically have nowhere else to go.

Hainan Island it is; China's only true tropical island destination, located at 17 degrees subtropical on your handy dandy GPS, directly across the middle of Vietnam.

In America, where the vacation-going middle class has a dozen nearby tropical choices such as southern California, Florida, the Bahamas, and Mexico, China has only one true tropical island destination—Hainan Island.

Specifically, the prime area is the stretch of oceanfront running from the west end of Sanya up the east coast to Boao, home of the annual ASEAN Forum. In addition, you have Haikou, the island capital city in the north. The beaches and winter weather are not as consistently nice as the southern end of the island but it's not bad.

Property Vacancy Rates

In a 2011 *Market Watch* article on Hainan, very well written by journalist Chris Oliver, it is mentioned that property vacancies down in Sanya are over 30%. This point is severely misunderstood. Apartments in Sanya are second homes, winter holiday homes, not a family's primary home, which is found up on the mainland.

They are normally vacant nine to ten months per year. I'm not saying real estate vacancy rates or overbuilding in China are not a concern. I am saying that the issue is much less meaningful regarding Hainan as a winter-time destination for Mainland Chinese. It's just a second home and it's most likely been paid for in cash. It will be passed on to the kiddies. Considering I spent my twenties and thirties living in the US dreaming as many do of buying a condo down in Mexico, I don't find anything bubbly about this state of affairs.

The scope of Hainan Island's tourism expansion is comparatively enormous. Existing International resort brands opened since the early 2000s. Though there are a few local brands, you will find that it is international chains that are catering to this wealthy set of Chinese.

Sheraton, Hilton, Marriott, Ritz Carlton, Pullman, Intercontinental, Crowne Plaza, Sofitel, and so many more. But what is truly amazing is the scale of projects that will be completed there by the end of 2012:

- Sheraton Haitang Bay (the island's third Sheraton after Sanya and Haikou)
- Starwood's Malus Luxury Collection Haitang Bay

- St. Regis Yalong Bay
- MGM Grand Yalong Bay
- Shangri La Haitang Bay
- Fairmont Haitang Bay
- Doubletree Haitang Bay
- Jumeirah Haitang Bay
- Raffles Haitang Bay
- Four Seasons Lu Hui Tou
- Pullman Sanya Bay (Pullman's second Hainan property)

. . . and that's just a "partial" list.

Development on Par

The new money in China has adopted many of the leisure products and pursuits from the West and Hainan is so packed with newly wealthy Chinese as well as an international travel destination that the island supports more than 30 golf courses. That's right, you could hit a different course every day for a month.

Located at the north side of the island province, Haikou is now holder of a Guinness Book of World Records. The Mission Hills golf community is home to a record 24 golf courses with all of the expected hotel and residential property development that one would expect goes along with such a project.

You can golf in Phoenix at the beautiful Orange Tree Golf Club for $40. On Hainan Island and all around China and Asia, green fees average $150 plus add-ons. It's an expensive leisure sport that Chinese are flocking to play.

Don't Mistake China's Opening Up as a Warm and Fuzzy Affair

Furthermore, the evidence is very clear that China is growing and expanding for the internal benefit of China and her citizens. While there are many comparisons between today's China expansion and the post-war expansion of the United States, don't make the mistake of thinking China's coming of age has the same ideology to become a welcoming multi-centric, international culture opening up to the world with open arms.

If anything, evidence exists they are starting to withdraw from the international stage in that many foreign companies and organizations consistently report that being present to do business in China is, if anything, getting harder not easier. International ties are driven strictly by government policy and business investment objectives.

The Beijing government still carefully controls its ideological borders, society, and culture as it deems fit to enable stability and harmony, not wanton American-style freedom. Needless to say, history brings much evidence that both approaches have their problems and challenges.

Oil's Future Reflected in China's Amazing Green Leap

Other countries are easily embarrassed by China's massive "green" revolution, a commitment with a magnitude far greater than any other country in the world including solar, wind, and nuclear energy. In demonstrating this commitment, they are also sending an amazing message on the future of energy: We truly don't want to need more and more oil and we are seriously committed to avoiding that problematic dependence. Here are the three reasons why, with the third being the big surprise.

Solar: China's commitment to solar energy is massive. From a recent article by Thomas Friedman, "Bill Gross, who runs eSolar, a promising California solar-thermal start-up: On Saturday, in Beijing, said Gross, he announced 'the biggest solar-thermal deal ever. It's a 2 gigawatt, $5 billion deal to build plants in China using our California-based technology. China is being even more aggressive than the U.S. We applied for a [US Department of Energy] loan for a 92 megawatt project in New Mexico, and in less time than it took them to do stage 1 of the application review, China signs, approves, and is ready to begin construction this year on a 20 times bigger project!'"

Wind Power: The situation is much the same regarding China's commitment to wind power energy. Blessed by the strong desert winds in Gansu Province, they are building numerous mega-sized wind farms totaling 20 megawatts of output by 2020, and at a third of the costs in the West. According to the Global Wind Energy Council, China has doubled its wind power capacity every year for the past five years.

China Goes Nuclear: Locally here in tropical Sanya, Hainan Island, China, I recently met a German who was a project manager in the nuclear industry in China. He told me they were working on the planning project to build 21 more nuclear power plants in the coming decade. The recent article by Thomas Friedman states China plans to build over 50 nuclear power plants by 2020. The fact is that most recent nuclear technology has become far more efficient and safe than the older nuclear equipment and planning that has been related to nuclear incidents.

According to hedge fund founder and market research pundit John Thomas, "The Middle Kingdom currently has 12 operational plants generating 12 gigawatts accounting for 2.3% of the country's power. Another 23 are currently under construction. It plans to add ten a year for the next decade, taking them up to 70 gigawatts by 2020, and a staggering 400 megawatts by 2050. That's nearly the total power generated in China today."

So then we have a clear picture of China's vision to significantly reduce its dependence on polluting fossil fuels, hoping of course that they will execute nuclear construction and development with state-of-the-art safety and technology protocols.

In the US, big oil and other special interest groups prevent nuclear from being a viable option on US soil. France has plenty of nuclear power and so does England. In comparison, what China has planned is truly a whole new level for the alternative energy industry. With China leading the way on this unexpected and unprecedented scale, the day will come when we may sarcastically wonder, Who needs oil?

Brief Highlights of China's Rising Wealth

For those of you who enjoy reading information in quick bites, let me present this set of highlights compiled from the ongoing research I have done. When organizations ask me to do a keynote talk on China, these are some of the highlights I typically work from in outlining the view on China's current and expected future wealth and society.

> " . . . 280 million—that's the total number of affluent consumers China is expected to have by 2020, more than doubling the current total of 120 million."
>
> ***
>
> " . . . most of China's current affluent population is under 45 years old . . . "
>
> ***
>
> " . . . The affluent will propel 40% of China's consumption growth . . . will comprise 35% of all consumer spending in 2020 . . . their spending will grow fivefold to $3.1 trillion in the next eight years."
>
> Above quotes from Boston Consulting Group
>
> ***
>
> Indra Nooyi, Pepsi's Global CEO has stated expectations for the global economy to hit 210 trillion by 2040 with a 40% share going to China.
>
> ***

Nobel Prize–winning economist Robert Fogel projects China's economy will soon dwarf America's, reaching a staggering $123 trillion. That's 40% of the global economy in 2040 versus 14% for America.

***

According to the IMF (International Monetary Fund), China will be #1 in GDP by 2017. And now you realize the reference is to "official" GDP.

***

The United Nations and Goldman Sachs both expect China's middle class to quadruple in size by 2020 to over 600 million. That's just the middle-class sector of the population.

***

According to reviews by McKinsey Insights China citing statistics from the US Census Bureau, in less than 15 years China's wealthy and upper-middle class combined will be twice the size of its US counterparts.

***

From China State Admin of Radio, Film & Television: In the first half of 2012, movie box offices in China reaped US$1.2 billion revenue, up 41.7% year on year, and import movie ticket sales were up 91.4%.

***

"Today's China has 2,800 shopping malls . . . How many shopping malls will China need? We did our calculations—15,000," according to Liew Mun Leong, president and chief executive of Singapore developer of CapitaLand, one of Asia Pacific region's dominant commercial real estate developers.

The China Shopping Center Development Association predicted that the number of shopping malls in China will likely exceed 7,000 by 2025, up from the existing 2,812. Association President Guo Zengli said that in 2011 alone, some 1,500 malls were being constructed in China.

***

Market research expert, Freedonia Group, on construction spending in China: Expected to rise by 9.4% each year through 2015, down from the rapid pace of expansion in the 2005–10 period . . . Expansion will be bolstered by a growing domestic economy, ongoing urbanization and industrialization, rebounding foreign investment funding, continuing efforts to expand and upgrade physical infrastructure, and rising income levels.

***

China has become the largest online retail market in the world, with the number of online shoppers reaching 210 million in June 2012, the First Financial Daily reported. Li Jinqi, director of IT at the Ministry of Commerce, said that China's e-commerce industry has expanded with over 30% annual growth.

***

Retail sales, one of China's major growth drivers, hit RMB 18.68 trillion (US$2.97 trillion) in the first 11 months of the year, growing 14.2% year-on-year, according to the National Bureau of Statistics (NBS).

***

(Reuters)—Dalian Wanda Group, the world's biggest owner of movie theaters, is in talks with leading Hollywood studios to co-produce films and is looking to buy and build hotels in major US cities . . .

*Bought US movie theater chain AMC Entertainment Inc. for $2.6 billion in September and has earmarked North America for $10 billion of deals over a decade . . .
*"And we're in negotiations with the city governments of Washington D.C., New York and other American cities for

> the construction of hotels, department stores and commercial properties."
>
> It was also recently announced in the major media sources that Dalian Wanda Group is starting cooperation on mega-projects with Reliance Group, one of India's largest real estate conglomerates.

***

In 2009, Chinese investment into Brazil totaled just US$300 million. One year later, this amount had risen to US$17 billion, heralding the beginning of perhaps one of the most rapidly developing trade relationships the world has ever seen.

As an example, Chery China Auto, one of China's top automotive companies is co-opening a factory in Brazil. So then, as we witnessed Hyundai and Kia showing up as new imports in the domestic US auto market, we now watch as China's prime auto brands land in new territories across the globe.

The Tax Puzzle

Ah, yes, death and taxes. We must ask the author, "Mario, as China modernizes the cash economy you speak of will start to shrink and the government will start collecting more taxes, don't you think?"

In a report published on December 12, the China Academy of Social Sciences (CASS) said the structural imbalance in the country's growth model, measured by its self-devised index, has significantly worsened over the past decade and more.

Separately, the research said the government's tax revenue has grown faster than GDP since 1997. Between 2000 and 2011, tax revenue as a share of GDP rose from 12.7% to 19%, while fiscal revenue, which includes tax, fees, and other administrative income, increased from 13.5% to 22%.

"Stepping up the strength of structural tax reduction is beneficial to reducing the burden of the economy and promoting enterprise investment and private consumption," the report said. It also noted that China should not levy high taxes to build a social welfare system that it can't afford.

And so in regards to the question asked, I can't imagine an answer other than, "Yes, that trend seems rather obvious." Yet another fascinating China–US dichotomy presents itself!

The US shadow cash economy, which hovers around $2 trillion, is actually increasing in size. This is in part driven by the number of long-term unemployed dropping off the list of reported unemployment claims and entering the shadow economy. And this trend exists within a society that is mature and saturated, now at the long end of its economic cycle.

As though a mirror opposite in every respect, *China's shadow economy of $6 to $10 trillion will decrease in size* as China modernizes and improves the efficiency of its tax revenue collections. Furthermore, China is economically at a far earlier stage in its economic development cycle.

Questioning the Wealth Gap

Let me summarize one of the most contentious and fiery fundamental economic issues in both the USA and China like this:

The elite rich have grabbed up a disproportionately massive chunk of the wealth. According to the Credit Suisse Global Wealth Databook for 2013, the top 8.4% of the world's population hold 83.3% of the wealth, totaling US$200 trillion. The rich are richer than ever and I mean obscenely rich and there is one iconic, straightforward statistic making it easy to see. Ten short years ago, Fortune 500 CEO compensation was around *42 times* average employee compensation. Today that ratio has multiple to a mind-boggling *367*. As such, it well represents the unfolding wealth gap soap opera, which rightfully upsets a lot of people. Our focus is to clarify reality not judge, so let's look deeper.

On the surface, the second part of the wealth gap narrative in China and the United States is quite different than common understanding leads us to believe. Even then, as we shall see next, there are glaring exceptions to the rule demanding rigor against the communication red flags of generalization, deletion, and distortion as we look at the wealth gap and related issues.

1. In the United States the lifestyle decline of the lower/middle class for the past two decades is apparent and well documented. While the rich have become obscenely rich, while corporate profits and cash on hand have soared to record highs, American middle-class wages have been flat for over ten years and the cost of living con-

tinues to rise. This is a well-known and straightforward picture of the situation.

2. In China, we have a different ballgame. Yes, we do know the rich have also become obscenely rich, yet the middle class has been enjoying the ride too. They also have experienced, in breadth and speed, a historically unprecedented rise in relative wealth and quality of life, as you by now well know.

(Speaking of quality of life, let's consider daily leisure lifestyle: when today's 30-something, big city Chinese were teens growing up, including my wife, they never went "shopping," not because they were poor or didn't feel like it but because there wasn't any! Families received their coupons to redeem at the store for their allotment of pork, rice, vegetables, and cooking oil. Leisure time was spent walking and at parks and gardens and reading books. There was no "Dad, can I have $20 so Johnny and I can go to the mall tomorrow?")

But then let's explain this next glaring discrepancy between such perceptions and reality. Here we will see where the money really does and doesn't trickle down from the top as we look at an aspect of the automotive industry.

A Luxury Car Purchase by the Numbers

A Mercedes Benz C-class sedan made in America and sold domestically in America has a sticker price of around $35,000. The American factory assembly worker who builds the car earns around $40 per hour.

A Mercedes Benz C-class sedan made in China and sold domestically in China has a sticker price at around $58,000. Wow, big price difference; it's 60% higher, and the reason is because China is a market of newly wealthy people who can both afford it and have availability in the market to buy it for the first time in their lives.

Yet the Chinese auto factory assembly worker who builds the car earns only around $10 per hour, one quarter of the American auto factory worker. Adding insult to injury, the price of the car is jacked up bringing even more revenue to the folks at the top off the economic pyramid.

This particular case reveals a socio-economic theme that falls way outside the common narrative of higher corporate profits vs. flat middle-class wages in America that we just reviewed. In this case, America's middle-class worker is earning a far *higher* percentage of the price of the car *and* the car is priced much lower so more people can afford to buy it. Meanwhile in China, the car has been intentionally positioned as an expensive, exclusive luxury for the rich with even higher profit margins while the factory worker earns far *less*.

Now let's look at another case in the restaurant/hospitality industry: Your $17 martini.

At a hot, swanky, five-star hotel or bar in the United States, you will pay $17 or more for a cocktail or beer. The person serving it to you earns around $100 per day.

Here in Shanghai, we find one of the coolest places on the planet to have a drink, the 90th-floor outdoor bar at the new Ritz Carlton Lu Jia Zui. Here, you will also pay the same price for that drink and receive the same quality of service.

The person serving the drink to you only earns around $15 a day, six times less.

So where is all that extra profit going? One answer is that the owners, the real estate developers, the big corporations—in other words, the rich people—are making it. A closer look at commercial retail business in China reveals lower wages but higher commercial rent rates. So, then, by this economic mechanism, the real estate developers, who are often state-owned enterprises or joint ventures, in other words the rich and powerful running the show, are hoarding the profits.

It all sounds quite familiar, doesn't it? A different twist on the same old story; the perpetual struggle for society to find the right balance and execution in the merits of capitalism and socialism.

The US National Export Initiative (NEI)

I am intentionally moving to the end of this writing on a positive note of caring, concern, and hope for the United States to overcome its own societal and economic challenges. I do so because it upsets me a lot and because many people expect that if an author puts forth issues and challenges in a given context, they should also provide a direction for moving forward into the future.

As that may be the case I can think of no better example than the case of the US National Export Initiative to make a big dent in aiding the US to solve its economic problems. I bring you this case with a tip of my hat to the US Chamber of Commerce Shanghai, which as the largest overseas US Chamber incessantly encourages Washington to improve relations and business with China. The good news is that they are making genuine progress.

> "Out of 435 [US] congressional districts, 249 of them had higher growth in exports to China last year than any other market in the world, according to the USCBC's 'Congressional District Exports to China' report . . . China wants what we produce. But they should want even more of it. The US lags behind the Europeans and Japanese in the Chinese market."
>
> *Forbes Magazine*, August 2013,
> "Why Hating China Is Futile," Kenneth Rapoza

According to the most recent reports, US exports are at an all-time high and exports to China are also at an all-time high. With every billion in exports creating 6,000 new US jobs, that's good news.

Let me drive the point home. Throwing in the common-sense view of marketing, you want to sell your stuff to who? Answer: the people who have the money!

Becoming newly aware that your target market is far more cash rich than you previously understood, wouldn't you fortify, tune, and clarify your plan?

And who do we know has lots more of that now? The Chinese; the highest-spending tourists, the ones with the most cash, the ones with the least amount of mortgage and credit card debt, and on top of all that, the ones who love American brands too!

So, America, get it together and embrace the opportunity that comes with all of these insights and ideas. As Mr. Rapoza well states in his *Forbes* article, "As this trend continues, hating China will be harder for politicians." If you have a product or service to sell, do your darnedest to figure out how to position yourself to be selling it to the folks who have money, which you now know includes a rising and expanding society of Chinese spreading across the world.

Life Stuck in the Mud? How About $20–$40 per Hour Cash Teaching English?

For those of you living simple lives with a high degree of frustration and nowhere to turn, what then do you have to lose if you allow yourself to realize you can make a change any time you want? If you have a reasonably nice personality and good communication skills, you can easily find a new life on a university campus in China teaching English to diligent, polite students who will respect you and call you "Laoshi," which is Mandarin for "teacher" or even "professor," while earning $20–$40 an hour plus a free apartment, holidays, and roundtrip airfare. You can do that for a year and then head back home if you don't wish to continue. Even in just that one year, you can easily sock $10,000 away in the bank.

The common objection is "I don't want to relocate." Okay, I get that and you may have many legitimate reasons why that is so. However, if that is not a complete block to making a change, then take a moment to assess in detail whether that is truly the case in your situation and relate it to the bigger picture of the history of mankind's migrations across the planet. From young people who are eager to study abroad for a year on university student exchange programs to many of our European ancestors who bravely immigrated to America for a better life, we can see that such a decision is not so unthinkable and may be the best decision you ever made. With today's Internet, you can easily and accurately Google search the key words.

And So . . .

The revelation that China has such trillions in an off-the-books cash economy leads us to hope that such a quiet strength and foundation in China's domestic consumer economy lends support to the economy and will act as a buffer against the other economic headwinds China faces.

None of us wants to see various existing trends in place to cause China's economy weaken. None of us wants to see the US economy weaken. One sneezes, the other catches a cold, and the entire global economy collectively feels it.

Even with the past few years of America's close-minded bias against China improving significantly, I still feel intimidated as an American saying positive things about China. I am an observer and if it walks like a duck and quacks like a duck, then it's a duck. I'm politically neutral due to my disdain for politics in general, and we all should rationally recognize that every country has a list of pros and cons to note.

I feel forced in today's political and media climate to state that in this book, my words are expressed strictly for the purpose of creating empathy and understanding and wisdom in others with respect among the countries of the world.

I confess that I am primarily an idealist, with the shadow of truth and integrity over me as I do my best to avoid any bias in my views one way or the other.

I do not love nor hate China, nor do I love nor hate America. I am sad as an American citizen to see the state of affairs that exists in the country that my great-grandparents came to more than a century ago in pursuit of the American ideal of freedom. I honor their courage and bravery and love for their family as they made such difficult decisions for themselves and their future generations, including for me.

There are aspects of both China and America that are advantageous, wonderful, and admirable. There are also things about living in China that I find deeply offensive, annoying, and unreasonable.

Both America and China have aspects to their cultures, people, and political systems that make any intelligent human being shake their head in wonder, disgust, and frustration. In both countries, people are engaged with daily values, beliefs, attitudes, and behaviors greatly influenced by the culture in which they live.

Is it preaching to suggest we need to understand our daily reality as it fits into the big picture; to see our lives, as accurately as possible, not clouded by personal or societal filters? Is it right to suggest we should not be pro- or anti-America nor pro- or anti-China? I believe it is good for our mental and emotional health. What I wish for myself as an author and for all of us as concerned brothers and sisters is to understand and interpret reality with a fair degree of accuracy and intelligence, to secure the future of our children for whom I am greatly concerned.

Please go travel. More meaningful than ever and easier than ever, one of the greatest gifts you can give yourself and give to your children is to travel to another country and enter the world of its people, to recognize more deeply what you do or don't like, to cause yourself to question your own assumptions. Considering our self-actualization as citizens of the world, I am certain that if we each spent a couple of years living in Italy, France, England, Spain, Saudi Arabia, India, Nigeria, the Philippines, or Japan, we would have a fascinating and diverse list of pros and cons and wows with respect to the culture, people, laws, and political systems of those countries.

And so, I am led to the deep conviction that we need to be wide awake, to embrace the oh-so-short, precious moment called life here on planet Earth; we can understand and be understood; enjoy, appreciate, and be appreciated; and, hopefully, make a meaningful contribution somewhere along the way.

We live in a breathtaking time in history, which urges us, requires us, dares us to open our eyes . . .

. . . to the big lies.

. . . to the little lies.

. . . to our own lies.

Part II

Unrepentant Scrutiny of Reality vs. Myth

"The response from our readers to Mario Cavolo's glowing take on China and the global economy was eye-opening, to say the least."

"Here's Mario with some thoughts on the subject that hit us like a bolt of lightning."

"The following essay provoked a firestorm in this forum, so it was run twice."

Rick Ackerman, *Rick's Picks*
Investment Advisory

***

"Mario's assessment of what is happening in China is spot on."

Ai Dehua, Forum Member, China
Expat resident

***

"Wow, Mario. Fascinating article. Most articles about the economy, I feel like I've read all the ideas before. But this is unique. Thanks so much for contributing, it gives me a lot to think about."

Jill Hotard, Clinical Psychologist, Seattle, WA

"Mario, I learn things here that I could never have learned otherwise; and you probably account for 90% of it."

Mark Uzick

Introduction to Part II

Part II of this book is not a continuation of the narrative found in Part I. Rather, here you will find a selected compilation edited and adapted from feature articles originally published on the website of US-based investment adviser Rick Ackerman. The author used this platform to share his unique insights with Rick's subscribers and now brings his experience and perspective to a wider audience.

Starting in October 2009, Cavolo was delighted to learn that his articles were welcomed for publishing by Acker-man, a financier who spent over a decade on the floor of the Pacific Coast Exchange, followed by work as a news-paper editor, journalist, and investigator including his work as a columnist for the *San Francisco Examiner* and contributor to *Barron's*. Through his newsletter, Rick challenges and informs some of the most intelligent and experienced traders on global economics and investing with his insightful, profound commentary on the state of international affairs.

This body of work reveals the author's views, as expressed to Ackerman's subscribers and followers, on the rise of Asia led by China and his unrepentant scrutiny of reality vs. myth. His mission is to insure that others have a clear and authentic understanding of what's really going on in China and what it may mean to them in their own lives.

This series spans a time frame beginning in the depths of America's financial crisis in October 2009 through to the end of 2012, marked by the US Federal Reserve Bank's Quantitative Easing programs, unrelenting economic woes in Europe, and China's unyielding defiance of ludicrous calls for the collapse of a real estate bubble—which actually doesn't even exist—by dreadfully uninformed media and economic pundits in the US and elsewhere.

It could be suggested that through this series of feature articles and the arguments that followed, Cavolo was forced to insure the integrity and accuracy of his reporting and views, as he often found himself facing responses from readers who were thoughtful yet seriously uninformed or misinformed regarding the situation in China. As the author's views have been known to provoke strong responses and fervent disagreement among some followers of the Ackerman forum, some articles are followed by a selection of further arguments between Cavolo and a number of newsletter subscribers, who possess a reputation for intelligence, passionate concern, and well-founded suspicion regarding the current state of economic and political affairs in the United States.

The author is not only outspoken upon matters in China. Included are some of his relevant and timeless insights into the global economy and markets from his unique perspective as a "fly on the wall" in China for more than a decade, an experience that sharpens contrasts between different nations, cultures, and markets. Time only further seals the accuracy and insightfulness of his views, and even though Ackerman occasionally raises strong counterpoints to Cavolo on certain issues, he will tip his hat to the power and freshness of these insights even if he does not always fully agree with the conclusions drawn.

The author challenges readers to ignore his macro-bullish view of China at their own peril. Many of those who are on the ground or truly "in the know" about China agree.

A "Fly on the Wall" Is Bullish on China (January 2010)

We put the knock on China the other day—not for the first time —in a commentary concerning Google's security problems there. This elicited a fascinating response from reader Mario Cavolo, a frequent contributor to the Rick's Picks *forum who lives and works in Shanghai as a motivational speaker. We asked him to expand his remarks, which cast China in a very bullish light. Here's what Mario had to say:*

—Rick Ackerman

Stop listening to the "bubble" doomsayers and pay attention to the realities of why China's expansion will continue for many years to come. My observations as a "fly on the wall" are a collective reflection of what I, as well as other foreign business people living here for five to ten years, have experienced.

The Mother of All Expansions

- China's expansion right now is quite similar to the post-WWII expansion in the US. It should be easy to recognize the parallels: inflation of consumer and real estate prices, the cost of doing business, continued asset inflation, and rising stock markets. These are all hallmarks of a country's economic and societal emergence.

- China's expansion is fired by huge supplies of a fuel called *cash*. We know about the trillions in the government sector. This is an amount well in excess of any projected debt levels in Beijing's budget. The *South China Morning Post*'s Tom Holland looked more closely at debt levels and potential bad loans that could boost total debt to a worst-case scenario of 55% of GDP, about the same as the UK. However, one must remember that the economy and tax revenues are growing solidly, and Beijing has no shortage of assets to set against its liabilities. So even with the concern over the GDP-to-government debt ratio, they *have* the *cash*—a crucial difference that makes China financially solid. Think of a corporation with $1 billion in debt but $2 billion in cash. It's solvent.

- China is embracing US-style capitalism and consumer spending is on the rise. Internally, the country's expansion is in an industrial boom stage. While America is at the other end of the cycle, the growth has just begun here and promises to continue for many years.

- Big business here—banks, insurance, energy, and more—got its start as big bureaucracy. While Americans are concerned about their government getting into banking and other businesses, in China the trend is going the other way, towards privatization through stock and bond offerings. Regarding the banks' level of services to account holders, my online account with ICBC is amazing: we are able to trade stock funds, gold funds, and physical gold, plus most major international forex pairs in online savings accounts round-the-clock.

- Foreign direct investment (FDI) continues to flow to Asia, with China leading the way. The crisis in the first half of 2009 short-circuited the global economy, but investment has almost returned to previous levels, with investors continuing to favor China. This, in spite of a European Commission annual report noting that it has become more difficult for foreign firms to enter the Chinese market! One of the reasons for this is that FDI tends to be long-term and therefore less affected by market fluctuations. These long-term investments are still in place and in a few years the 2008 "Global Economic Meltdown" that did not seem so global in China will be all but forgotten—and these investments will be paying dividends.

- Road construction, to accommodate the country's automobile boom, has also been spectacular, much like the construction of the US Interstate Highway System in the 1950s. You can't travel anywhere in China without seeing the ribbons of multi-lane expressways stretching into the distance, with concrete pillars ready to support the elevated highways that will soon crown them. The scale of this expansion is simply mind-boggling—and wherever this expansion happens, the value of the real estate doubles or triples and a boom in local construction occurs.

In 2006, Jiangsu Province, in an "if we build it, they will come" bid for prosperity, made a policy to connect every village with paved roads. Some villages not so far from town were so cut off by lack of infrastructure that a decision to go the few kilometers into the nearest town might take half a day. Thousands of kilometers of dirt tracks were suddenly paved with at least a single-lane cement roadway. So what if one car needs to pull off to let another pass? It sure beat muddy, potholed dirt roads that bicycles could barely navigate and most motorized vehicles shunned to travel if they valued their suspensions. Though the government decision was based more on push than demand, do you think this increased the speed of business and created new stimulus and new opportunities? You bet.

Real Estate Bubbles "Limited"

- I mention above that infrastructure investments have been increasing the property values, both in major cities as well as in rural areas. Rising real estate prices are a phenomenon of the time, no different than that experienced during similar cycles in the US and Europe. Exorbitant bubble-price problems exist only in limited areas, with more reasonable price increases occurring in second- and third-tier cities that have a well-developed middle class. For example, in Shenyang, Liaoning Province, a booming second-tier city, apartment prices are now averaging US$70–120 per square foot. Does that sound like a bubble?

- A rising stock market. Admittedly, market prices are peaky—but again, we need to remember that this is a market not fueled by debt, but by government and private sector cash in an unprecedented regional expansion where power is constantly shifting.

- Debt levels far lower than in the West. Starting with a decade of 36% savings rates, we can begin to grasp the amount of cash in the private sector—similar to Japan, even amongst the lower and middle classes in China. Relatively speaking, the cost of living has been three to five times lower than in the US or Europe, including the cost of real estate. That is why until now there has been very little mortgage and credit card debt amongst the citizenry. With the current real estate boom pushing prices toward Western levels, mortgaged properties still comprise far less than half of purchased properties, and those properties that are mortgaged require a 30% down payment. In addition, bank credit card marketing is literally a new industry, with banks only starting to encourage "plastic" in the past two years.

Real Jobs

Pay close attention to this comparison between low-level jobs in China and the US. It paints a realistic picture of typical employment for low-to middle-income workers/managers working for a Chinese company (multinationals pay much higher salaries):

- These workers generally see low salaries, roughly equivalent to US minimum wage. For example, a restaurant or hotel department manager may earn a monthly salary in the range of US$300–700, plus a year-end bonus equal to two or three months' pay.

Now ask yourself this question: What would America be like, what would life be like for lower/middle-class families earning minimum wage across America if companies also offered the following comprehensive perks:

- Bus transportation: You are picked up and dropped off as needed for your shifts.

- Arrive at work and eat breakfast: Three meals a day in your company's on-site cafeteria where workers and management eat together. If there is a daily cost to the meals deducted from your pay, it is at a rock-bottom price.

- Housing: Dormitory rooms are shared by two to six workers, depending on their level of employment, and private apartments for managers. This may be a locally leased, 3–4 bedroom private apartment, or a large dormitory facility housing hundreds of workers campus-style at the work site.

- Full medical coverage: Medical expenses in China are dirt cheap even without insurance. In case you are wondering about quality, over the past twelve years, I have often gone to Chinese hospitals for care and received reasonable, intelligent care. More on that in a separate chapter; our focus right now is on costs. For example, a normal visit to the hospital costs US$2 for a doctor visit, US$5 for Zithromax, US$10 for X-rays, US$10 for various blood tests, US$50 for a CT scan and US$100 for an MRI. Foreign friends I know have had very satisfactory hernia operations for no more than US$1,500, all inclusive, and none of them had a single complaint.

- Paid "golden week" national holidays three times per year: Labor Day in May, National Day in October, and Spring Festival/Chinese New Year, falling in January or February.

- Paid overtime or triple time: By Chinese law, if you work on an official holiday, you receive three additional paid holidays or triple-time pay.

- Maternity leave: By law, when a woman gets pregnant in China, she has several weeks to six months of maternity leave and a guarantee that she can return to her job afterwards.

Chinese employment is certainly not perfect, but it is secure and stable. Compare it to a typical job at Walmart, where an American makes minimum wage, but pays taxes and his or her own rent, transportation costs, and meals. The Walmart worker is in much worse shape than a typical Chinese making US$500 per month who still banks 50% of his paycheck because his living expenses are so low.

Going Green

- China has figured out that the nations that have energy independence will have a distinct advantage in coming years and they have committed heavily to renewable energy. They also have the manufacturing scale to initiate green energy production from the world's largest hydroelectric projects to massive wind farms and solar arrays; natural gas; LPG; *and* 50 new nuclear plants. The Shanghai taxi company runs its fleet of 50,000 Volkswagens on LPG! Did anyone outside of China know that? For more details on wind, solar, and nuclear, read on.

- China's commitment to solar energy is massive. Here's a relevant excerpt from a *New York Times* column by Thomas Friedman*: "Bill Gross, who runs eSolar, a promising California solar-thermal start-up . . . announced 'the biggest solar-thermal deal ever. It's a 2 gigawatt, US$5 billion deal to build plants in China using our California-based technology. China is being even more aggressive than the US. We applied for a [US Department of Energy] loan for a 92 megawatt project in New Mexico, and in less time than it took them to do stage one of the application review, China signs, approves, and is ready to begin construction this year on a 20 times bigger project!'"

- The situation is much the same regarding China's commitment to wind power. Blessed with strong desert winds in Gansu Province, they are building numerous mega-sized wind farms totaling 20 megawatts of output by 2020, and at a third of the costs in the West. Accor-ding to the Global Wind Energy Council, China has doubled its wind power capacity every year for the past five years.

- Though you might debate me on whether you see this as "green" or not, China is going nuclear, mines its own nuclear resources in the mineral-rich desert near the western capital city of Lanzhou, and will be drastically reducing its reliance on coal and oil. Locally, here in tropical Sanya on Hainan Island, I recently met a German who was a project manager in China's nuclear sector. He told me they were working on a plan to build 21 more nuclear power plants in the coming decade. The recent article by Friedman states China plans to build more than 50 nuclear power plants by 2020.

- Public transit: Typically, there are half a dozen sub-ways and ten bus routes at each bus stop throughout the city. In addition, there are tens of thousands of electric scooters and bicycles along the roads. Bottom line, a typical Chinese does not need a car to get to their workplace, and as pointed out, much of the taxi fleet runs on LPG, as do many buses. Additionally, there is a network of electric buses as well, reducing the pollution levels of 20 million souls on their daily commute.

- The expansion of infrastructure recalls America in the postwar years. There is massive expansion of subways and high-speed rail. I'm talking half a dozen new sub-way lines being added in each city, not just one or two, and high-speed rail lines that will soon connect all major cities at 300+ kph. They won't need as much oil for airplanes when high-speed train travel is a widespread option. It is easy to identify these projects by typing in the keywords on-line. Numerous high-speed lines have opened this past year with the major Beijing-Shanghai line covering 1,300 km in less than five hours instead of the former fourteen hours. The US could learn from China in this respect.

Main Street Business

- Indicator: My email box is repeatedly loaded with AmCham Shanghai job messages and position offers. But let's be clear here that things have changed. Ten years ago, being a foreigner here might have been a ticket to success by itself. Now, almost all of these many job opportunities require that you be totally fluent in Mandarin Chinese or have a very specialized and advanced level of expertise that they cannot get locally.

- Indicator: My friends who are consultants and trainers say their budgets have recovered in the last four months. If business is bad, the first thing companies cut are outsourced services like these.

- Discretionary consumer spending is also on a major upswing. For example, since autos are not needed to hold a job as they are in the US, the amazing automobile boom is totally vanity driven. They are just the newest, greatest, modern addition to the nouveau lifestyle they have discovered and crave here, along with iPhones, LCD TVs, and other consumer gizmos. A population of more than 200 million Chinese are new members of the middle class, eagerly intent on enhancing their lives with American-style vanities of the 1980s. Remember, they still have almost no credit card debt or mortgages.

So stop wondering how things are in China, because you are receiving this information from a "fly on the wall." Let this picture of Chinese reality sink in. Spread the word, and plan accordingly. It is going to be a rough ride, but China is doing fine internally—or, I should say, well enough.

Another huge point I'd like to address is about insurance industry-related costs, which are much lower here. There are so many systemic insurance expenses in the US that don't exist here; the hell of tort law with outrageous payouts and premiums that have brought the US to its knees are an issue that China doesn't have to deal with. Insurance premiums and liability payout levels, awards, and punitive damages are much, much lower.

I also feel there is a need to clarify some issues regarding real estate and income:

- The lower income strata are surely left behind, same as in the US. People earning minimum wage definitely can't afford to buy a home.

- However, the extreme bubble price range of US$300–750 per square foot is limited to the first-tier cities of Shanghai, Shenzhen, Guangzhou, and Beijing, plus a handful of others.

- Take my sample case of Shenyang, one of China's second-tier cities—US$70–120 per square foot is the pricing for very nice, new apartment complexes, mid- to luxury-level. For instance, the Riverside Landmark complex next to the new golf course on the river is luxury-level (marble covers everything, etc.) with asking prices at US$133 per square foot. Mid-level quality Pan China Apartments, with a Walmart downstairs, half a kilometer from the Olympic Stadium, has asking prices at US$80 per square foot. Remember though this is for the "bare shell." You still have to decorate the entire interior. This will run an additional US$15–50 per square foot, depending on the quality level you choose.

- Kohn Pederson Fox, designers of the new Mandarin Oriental at City Center Las Vegas, has designed a similar multi-use City Center under construction in Shenyang now. Serviced apartments there will surely be at least twice as much as the Riverside Landmark—about US$270 per square foot.

- Older, normal, local walk-up apartments in second-tier cities have gone up in price from US$15 per square foot to the US$30–$45 per square foot range.

- Rents in older local apartments are US$140–200 per month. For the newer, luxury apartments mentioned rents are $250–450 per month.

A Day in the Life of a Shanghai Consumer (March 2012)

We recently asked our friend Mario Cavolo, a frequent contributor to the RICK'S PICKS *forum, what it's like from a cost-of-living stand-point to live in Shanghai. A New York City expatriate who lives and works in Shanghai himself as an entrepreneur, author, and TV and radio personality, he graciously obliged with the guest commentary below. The fictitious diary below is of a middle manager, Mr. Wang, who like many of us in the US, struggles to make ends meet.*

—Rick Ackerman

In this piece, we shall spend an imaginary and obviously unrealistic day in the life of a typical middle-class man living an ordinary life in Shanghai. In the process, we shall come to better understand the typical costs associated with middle-class family life in today's China. Our "average Joe" is Mr. Wang, 30 years old, a white-collar worker who might be an engineer, architect, human resources administrator, or account manager. He is a middle-class professional who works for a large Chinese or multinational company, earning a salary of perhaps RMB 4,000–8,000 (US$670–$1,340) per month plus a nice benefit package, and lives "in the city" with his wife and cousin. Note as well that if the Wang family lived in a second-tier city such as Chengdu, Shenyang, Changchun, and dozens of others, the local costs and prices noted would range 20%–40% lower. For example, a taxi in Shanghai starts at RMB 14 (US$2.20), whereas in Shenyang they start at RMB 8 (US$1.40). Similar local apartment rents in a second-tier city are quite low, at RMB 1,500–2,500 (US$275–$450) per month for a 2–3 bedroom unit.

Mr. Wang's Rough Morning

Sunrise greets us once again, leading us out the door at eight a.m. from Wang's 900-square-foot, 3-bedroom, third-floor walk-up, which rents for RMB 3,000 (US$500) per month. Mind you, that is pretty cheap, but only because Mr. Wang does not live in prime downtown Shanghai, where rent for the same type of older apartment would be closer to RMB 5,000 (US$800). Note that I did say three bedrooms, as Mr. Wang's cousin lives in the third. This type of sharing is the rule, not the exception, in China, leading me to tell you that I estimate the average range for rent per person to be RMB 625–1,350 (US$100–200) per month.

It is a briskly paced ten-minute walk to the subway or public bus, which awaits at a cost of RMB 5 (US$0.50) for a 30–40 minute transit to work; Wang makes a five-minute breakfast pit stop along the way at one of many street vendors selling RMB 2 (US$0.25) veggie- or meat-filled steam buns or a Chinese-style fast-grilled pancake with an egg in it, along with a container of milk or soy milk at RMB 1.5 (US$0.20). He checks his watch on arrival and exclaims, "Wa! I'm running late!" so instead of walking, he hops on the back of one of the many (illegal) motorcycle taxis or tricycle carts for RMB 5 (US$0.50) to arrive at work in five minutes instead of the usual fifteen. Alternately, Wang could live it up a bit and hop a taxi to work every morning for RMB 30 (US$5). Better yet, if Wang is fortunate enough to work for one of the many regional or national-sized companies who offer shuttle bus pickup/drop-off every hour from 8 a.m. to 10 p.m., the cost of his commute drops to zero. That's quite a benefit, as a result of which Mr. Wang's main means of transportation in his personal life is an old, rusty bicycle, which he won't replace with a new one because a new one is more likely to be stolen—no car is necessary.

A Toothache Strikes!

Nine a.m., and agony strikes! "Arghh! My toothache has returned," exclaims Mr. Wang to his boss—and off he goes for a root canal at a local, clean, decent dental clinic. The price? US$85 for the typical three-visit root canal. On the way back to the office, Wang decides to stop at the local Circle K-type market where it is convenient to pay his utility bills and charge up his mobile phone (US$10–20 per month). His average monthly utility bill—gas, electricity, and water—is close to RMB 180 (US$30) or RMB 1,000 (US$120), depending. Say what? Well, yes, depending. You see, if Wang is a typically thrifty local Chinese living south of the mighty Yangtze River, he wears lots of thick clothes in the winter, when temperatures average 4–10°C/35–40°F, with perhaps a couple of weeks at or below zero, and he doesn't need to turn on the heat—nor would he think of doing so. In fact, even the student dormitories at Shanghai's best universities are not heated in the wintertime, only the dorm's bath/shower areas get that luxury. And no, as you are surely about to ask, the students are not allowed to bring in little electric space heaters to get toasty. Ditto for summertime heat, many Chinese will relieve the heat of humid 35°C/90°F days with no more than the breeze of electric and hand-held fans.

Ten a.m., and more agony! Wang's cousin went out the door at the same time this morning to do the day's shopping at the local farmer's market. He spent RMB 3 (US$0.50) per pound for a typical assortment of veggies such as lettuce, peppers, potatoes, leeks, and onions, RMB 9 (US$1.50) per pound for a variety of fresh clams, RMB 20 (US$3) for two pounds of fresh or frozen perch, RMB 35 (US$5.75) for a live, two-pound catfish, or double that price for a cut of the day's salmon carcass. Hankering for meat, he sauntered over to the butcher's area and picked up some pork loin with a thick strip of fat still on its edge at RMB 18 (US$3) per pound and raw chicken for RMB 12 (US$2) per pound. Chicken breasts, incidentally, are equally cheap, as they are not regarded as a higher-quality meat cut compared to legs and thighs because the breast meat is regarded by the Chinese as tougher and dryer.

Grocery Mishap

Moving back to the agony in the story, on the way back home from the market Mr. Wang's cousin slipped in a puddle of water along the curb and, wow, you should have seen the groceries go flying! Sad to see all that food hit the ground, only some of which could be saved. But more to the point, Wang's cousin's lower back also hit the ground with a thud, and so off to the hospital he went.

Eleven a.m., and we arrive at Dong Fang #1 Hospital on the Pudong side of Shanghai's Huangpu River. If you happened to need to park your car, that'll be RMB 10 (US$1.50) (note: #1 level hospitals are the larger, main city hospitals, rather than smaller local #2 and #3 hospital clinics, which also exist in China's healthcare system. They offer many services that smaller hospitals do not, as they have better diagnostic equipment.) The fee at the patient registration window comes to RMB 20 (US$3.50)—when was the last time your copayment was that low? The nurse asks, "What's the problem?" Wang's cousin replies, "I fell, lower back/hip injury." He's sent to the third floor, room 15C, and instructed to wait there until they call his name. Now, mind you, this is similar to a doctor's visit in the West where you wait in the waiting room until they call you or your number lights up on an LED board to tell you it's your turn. Except that you did not need to make an appointment in the first place. Furthermore, if Wang's cousin's injury was more of an emergency that could not wait, he would have gone directly to the emergency department, where he would presumably be seen sooner, but at essentially the same cost.

It's now 11:30 a.m. Sorry, pal. W-a-a-a-y too many people at the hospital today, so you'll be seeing the doctor after lunch. A truly local Chinese lunch typically consists of some meat, fish, or tofu with veggies over rice and costs the average local RMB 8–15 (US$1.25–2.50). For those Chinese citizens guilty of creating the new generation of unhealthy fat kids, a McDonald's or KFC meal combo with fries and a Pepsi goes for RMB 15–25 (US$2.50–$4). Those on tight budgets will eat two or three stuffed steam buns at RMB 2 (US$0.20) each. Oh, and don't forget the fresh fruit! RMB 1 (US$0.15) for that "apple a day . . . "

Afternoon Shopping Spree

The doctor gets around to seeing Wang's cousin at 2:30 p.m. He's pretty sore, so the doctor orders an X-ray, writes it up, and hands the slip to Wang's cousin who goes to pay at the cashier's window on the second floor. The cost? RMB 45 (US$7.50). He waits for the radiology department to hand him the S-ray envelope so he can take it upstairs to the doctor. Note on payment for services: Whatever the doctor at the hospital orders, whether a test or blood work—or an X-ray—you pay for it first or you don't get it. Also, if you have medical benefits as part of your employment package, typically you are given a plastic company debit card on which is a credit of a few hundred RMB for you to use when you need to see a doctor or buy medicine.

It seems Wang's cousin really whacked his lower back, so now the doctor orders a CT-scan, priced at RMB 300 (US$45). The scan is somehow still not able to satisfy this meticulous doctor, so he orders an MRI! Good grief! Mortgage the house! Sell the dog! Just kidding, folks. What's this really going to cost? Around RMB 800 (US$130). That's without insurance, and not kidding. (I've had two of them myself.) Finally, we hear from the doctor: "Wang's cousin is okay. He will survive!" the physician declares. But his convalescence will require plenty of ibuprofen—not so cheap at RMB 17 (US$3) for a box of 20 twelve-hour 300 mg capsules—and ice over the next two weeks. There was a break of the skin that wasn't too deep, but just to be safe the doctor gives Wang's cousin a prescription for some ciprofloxacin, um, oh shoot, or was that cephalexin? Darn, I can't remember, but I do remember the week's cost of those handy-dandy antibiotics at a dirt cheap RMB 15 (US$2.50)! Now, this next part is really embarrassing and a bit of a side story. I heard through the grapevine that Wang's aunt's sister-in-law's best friend, Miss Ding, is really fuming these days because she dated Wang's cousin's other friend for a couple of months and now finds herself with a case of herpes! Ho-ho. Gossipy stuff in deed, but I mention it only because a typical ten-day course of acyclovir probably sets the poor girl back a scant RMB 50 (US$8.75).

Harvard-Trained MD

Did I mention that Wang's cousin was chatting with the doctor during the exam? In fact, the doctor spoke decent English and enjoyed practicing with Wang's cousin, who wasn't half bad at English himself. Wang's cousin asked, "Ah, you have been to the US, really? Where?" The doctor replied, "Massachusetts! I studied at Harvard Medical School." Not bad for a US$3.50 hospital registration fee, eh?

Meanwhile, Wang's cousin's friend Li was kind enough to come to the hospital so Wang could get back to work. Li drives a decent car and stops at the gas station for 20 liters of 93 octane regular at RMB 8.5 a liter, which I believe is around US$5 a gallon. This friend of the Wang family is also a smoker, and, as the story reveals, quite the compulsive shopper as well! He picks up a fresh pack of the famous Double Happiness brand cigarettes at RMB 5 (US$0.90) while there are a variety of other brands running from three to ten times higher in price depending on whom you might be trying to impress. Thirst suddenly comes, so the cold section door swings open as a hand grabs plastic pints of Coke, green tea, and spring water, all priced around RMB 3 (US$0.35). Ooh, man! Mid-day, low-sugar hunger pangs hit, and so it's time for a quick-food snack like fast-food Japanese rice rolls stuffed with veggie, tofu, and that fake-crab stuff. Cost: another RMB 6 (US$1). As you will have surmised by now, the average Chinese diet isn't much healthier than an average American diet, with too many carbs and fats. And yet, people here are slimmer, perhaps because walking and biking are much more common.

Happy-Hour Libations

Of course, Wang's cousin's friend would never drink alcohol before driving because the law in China has zero tolerance for alcohol in your blood while driving, and a violation earns one a guaranteed 15 days in detention plus a one-year driver's license suspension. So with that sobering thought in mind, he picks up a few to take home; Budweiser, as well as Japanese brands Asahi and Kirin (all at 4% alcohol) go for RMB 8 (US$1.40) per pint, while the famous local brews like Tsingdao and Snow (at 2–3% alcohol) go for half that price at only RMB 4 (US$0.70) per pint. To liven things up a bit and keep warm in the winter without heat, cheap, 80–100 proof rice liquor rocket fuel called "baijiu" is also available for less than a buck.

For those who drink alcohol, we must pause to note that here's where the alcohol thing gets crazy: wine. You see, Wang's cousin's friend Mark is a foreigner from France. He's coming for dinner tonight and we don't need to speculate on whether he prefers wine with dinner. Nothing fancy, even a decent Chilean merlot will do, Mark reminded his host a couple days earlier. Back in the US, as you know, it's off to

Trader Joe's, where you'll find a lovely variety of drinkable wines from US$5–12 per bottle. And in fact, you'll find the same variety and selection of the world's most popular wines in Chinese supermarkets, too: Chilean, Australian, French, South African, Californian, and, hey, you can bet the Italian Pinot Grigios and Chiantis are right there too. Glorious days for the nouveau Chinese wine consumer!

Explosive growth in the wine market has arrived in China—indeed, right along with explosive consumption growth of most goods, imported or otherwise. Except that a bottle of the cheapest drinkables here will set you back around triple—at least RMB 80–120 (US$13–20)—and most of the nicer, middle-of-the-road bottles that would run US$15–30 back in the US or Europe will set you back a cool RMB 250–500 (US$40–90) here! Of course, when you're in the mood to indulge and impress once a week (as Wang's cousin's friend is obliged to do for his house guests), there's nothing like an imported bag of Doritos, which will set you back a cool RMB 60 (US$9.50), to go with that US$30 bottle of rot-gut French table merlot.

From Grapes to Italian Tomatoes

Grapes and tomatoes are said to be very healthy, both packed with all those micronutrients such as lycopene and others that I won't bother to mention here. I bring it up because, while consumer goods imported from most other countries like the US, Australia, or other European countries are typically double or triple the cost, Italian imported goods are not. As a typical Italian-American growing up in New York, canned Italian plum tomatoes were a staple, along with garlic and olive oil. Here in China, those imported cans of Italian tomatoes, along with Italian pastas and a few other Italian imported products (except all olive oils, which are also expensive), are priced no higher than back in the States. A can of Italian plum tomatoes here sets Wang back RMB 12 (US$2), a bargain for those times when his foreign friends come for dinner, giving Wang and his lovely wife a chance to try their hand at cooking Western foods for a change.

It's a Boy!

9:00 p.m.—Aya! (the Chinese version of Wow! or Gee!): Wang's wife's water broke after dinner! Off to the Pudong #1 Maternity Hospital they go for an uncomplicated, natural childbirth, three nights of rest, and another happy family joins China's current boom-boom baby boom that no one besides me seems to be noticing and writing about.

More to the point for today, let's talk about the pregnancy and birth bill. Mrs. Wang is a tiny thing, and so, while her baby was healthy, but at 32 weeks still a bit "on the small side," the doctor recommended that Mrs. Wang do what I call the "Chinese pregnant mother cheap country club hospital holiday." This means sharing a room with three to five other expecting mothers, there to relax, eat well, receive extra protein, amino acids, and vitamins by IV, and receive one round (one round regarded as quite safe) of dexamethasone to insure the healthy development of the wee one's lungs. As to the cost of this rather common event in the world of Chinese families: seven days in the hospital, shared room, at an average of RMB 700 (US$110) per day, totaling RMB 5,000 (US$980).

Wow, a decent medical-themed holiday! Now add in half-a-dozen routine hospital follow-up visits with ultrasounds and blood tests during the term of the pregnancy, at an average of RMB 300 (US$75) per visit. Finally, the bill for the labor/birth experience typically comes in at China's largest, most popular maternity wards around RMB 6,000 (US$1,000). Pudong's #1 Maternity, however, is regarded as a step-up in quality from most, so the final bill is higher at RMB 11,000 (US$1,600). Again, all of my costs noted are without any type of health care coverage.

Drugs, Gambling and . . . Baby Formula

Considering the baby boom currently under way here, it is fitting that our look at middle-class costs ends at the beginning—the beginning of family life, that is. A month's worth of comfy diapers dings the daily budget for around RMB 9 (US$1.50) per day, totaling RMB 270 (US$45) per month—not much cheaper than in the states, I suspect (six to eight diapers per day, right, dads?). China's baby car seats—which, by the way, are still not required by law—can be purchased for around RMB 300 (US$50) and you'll need RMB 250–500 (US$40–$80) for a decent China-brand stroller.

No story such as this can touch well upon the concerns and needs of today's Chinese families without exploring the hottest product around—one for which Chinese people cross the border by the thousands into the gambling Mecca of Macau each and every day. Drugs? No. You mean, gambling? Nope. You must mean the prostitutes then?! Wrong again. It's baby formula, a food product in a country with a dismal record of food manufacturing safety, a topic laced with legitimate worry, and a product hopefully never again laced with melamine. Reputable Chinese-brand baby formula will set back the Wang family budget by about RMB 625 (US$100) per month. You should know that this is an item where many families will, if at all possible, buy the more trusted, better brands and even imported brands of baby formula, raising the wallet-shrinking number to well over RMB 1,000 (US$150) per month.

Last time I checked, in every country and culture around the globe, mama's breast milk was still absolutely free. Thankfully, there are some sacred things in this world that the shenanigans of today's shameful politicians, greedy banking elite, and even China's highly inflationary economy simply can't touch.

Rising Asia Will Soften West's Economic Decline (June 2012)

From his new headquarters in a fashionable district of Shanghai, our friend and frequent contributor Mario Cavolo, a communications consultant, recently surveyed the passing parade. Bullish thoughts on the global economy ensued. For, who can doubt the dawning Asian century will help balance out the difficulties that seem likely to hobble the economies of the West? For an uplifting, long-term view with a global perspective, read his essay below.
—*Rick Ackerman*

Does it not occur to any pessimist that a massive region of the world is expanding, not contracting, and that this statistical fact portends well for the future demand of all "stuff" across the globe? While assuredly not discounting disturbing global financial and economic pressures, pessimists and permabears seem to relish discounting the powerful, upward expansionary forces across the global economy that also clearly exist.

Here in Shanghai, I now sit in the new upper-middle class mall called Kerry Parkside, where we have a marketing location for our various services. Forget the fact that prices are annoyingly high and that the mall is still packed on the weekends. Let's consider right now only the part of the story that gives us a glimpse of the future:

Observing every family that enters this mall, every woman I see is either with a baby/toddler in tow or pregnant. Did I say "every"? Apologies. Of course not, and I readily confess such an exaggeration. Yet it boggles my mind to note how many pregnant women and children under three years old there are here, appearing very much as the rule, not the exception. The same exact observation is easily made across China's 20 or so major urban centers, now totaling a population well over 300 million.

Ladies and gentlemen, embrace and gladly welcome the greatest baby boom in history, unprecedented in world history, size, and scope, far beyond America's relatively miniscule post-war baby boom. Similar stories of expansion in Latin America also tell the global story. They will need to consume plenty of "stuff," is that correct? There will be a resulting demand for response to the challenges their presence on the globe creates—more services, more solutions, more needs, more issues, more responses, more infrastructure, more food, more investment, more issues, more solutions, more and more demand of everything for more and more people.

Overbuilt? Hardly . . .

You say China's infrastructure is overbuilt? Tell that to a telecommunications industry serving more than 900 million mobile users, or to an automotive industry that is cranking out one million cars per month for sale both domestically and to the rest of the world. Tell me, all those roads somehow don't need to be built? How can one reach such a naive, short-sighted conclusion? Similar stories emanate from India and Latin America, do they not?

To which we next hear the "they already over-expanded and overbuilt" argument. Once again, short-sighted. What timeframe are you referring to? See past Wall Street's shameful focus on the quarterly earnings and set your sights instead on building a country for the long-term future; for the 40 million cars that will be coming; for an additional 200 million urban workers; for families who will need a place to live in the few supposed "ghost towns" that are often wrongly associated with the collapse of the Chinese real estate market.

Let us also digress a moment to note very similar stories of expansion across Asia, across the other BRIC emerging economies, so as to not overplay the China-centric view of these matters.

A Vast Grey Market

America spent the last 70 years extending its dominion over all things cultural and financial. Now it is China's turn. China is very different for reasons that are easy to both observe and measure, exhibiting realities that Westerners too easily forget or simply cannot comprehend. Every scary report about municipal debt, for one, is offset by the uncounted trillions of renminbi in China's grey market economy, well documented by a 2011 Credit Suisse report*. Should we overlook this? Not when we realize that 90% of Chinese own their homes, most of them mortgage-free. Not when we realize that amongst those one million shiny new cars hitting the road each month, the vast majority have been purchased with cash. Do you think that the majority of those cars are pricey US$100,000 Mercedes-Benzes, Audis, or BMWs—or are they US$12,000–25,000 models being purchased by the middle class? You know the answer, and yet it's hard to swallow it because here in China, when talking with a typical, first-time, middle-class car buyer, we ask, "Nice, how much did you pay for your new car?" In the West, our first question is, "What's your monthly payment?" Giggle.

Global Troubles Loom

Indeed, as Rick Ackerman sometimes reminds us, these newly arrived citizens of the world will be paying higher and higher prices for the future goods and services they are consuming. That much is true, and inflation over decades is nothing new. However, I would argue that the world's sovereign financial problems will be managed in a way that allows inflation to continue as a release valve and that, furthermore, the doomsday scenario is relative rather than absolute (as in, "The banking system must collapse!"). Clearly, it is relatively worse for the West at the end of a 60-year economic cycle, compounded by overreaching, elitist banking lunacy and unbridled Wall Street corruption. And yet, such factors are unlikely to have as much of an impact on emerging Asian and Latin American regions thanks to their fundamentally rising, expanding societies.

One can therefore be certain that as Europe and America deal with their appalling financial issues, China over the next several decades will extend its cultural and financial influence in the way that America's post-war expansion did over a period of 70 years. In either case, we must live with outcomes, whether good or bad.

China May Say Adios

There is one other, more dire possibility to ponder that China's leaders may ultimately choose as they have in the past. If the West truly implodes, China, able to flourish economically on its own, may forego global bargain hunting and shut its doors, isolating itself as the Middle Kingdom once again. Considering how far the country's political and economic reach has grown to date, that is possible but not likely. As a telling indicator, however, we must note that over the past two years, the business environment for foreign companies has deteriorated and become less welcoming.

For the past 50 years, the West has held sway economically. Now there will be a painful rebalancing across the globe, with the West's economic strength leaching into a rising Asia led by China. Meanwhile, we can easily agree that Rick Ackerman is right—that the next ten years, or perhaps much sooner, could see a mind-boggling financial upheaval caused by a collapsing financial system. But that is still a very short-term view. Perhaps it is an opportunistic way of seeing things for nimble traders, bond vigilantes, elitist bankers, hedge funds, and other short-termers exhibiting the best and worst attributes of the capitalist system simultaneously. Yet, recovery and restructuring will follow, built on the demand of the very real, unprecedented boom across the powerful, emerging economies of which I speak.

Middle Class Boom

Related to the baby boom demand theme of the article, I read a report that included the statement, "according to Goldman Sachs and the UN, China's middle class will be approximately four times that of the US middle-class population within one generation."

Perhaps this helps us to understand why GS is ramping down its Western presence and massively ramping up its Asia-based operations and investment interests. Further, according to the National Bureau of

Statistics of China released by McKinsey Global Institute, compared to most developed markets, the higher earners of this rising middle class will be uncommonly young. Of course we can understand that China needs to success-fully push itself up the value chain to sustain this growth.

Another indicator? From BBC News: "Volkswagen record car sales ... 5.1 million cars worldwide, 1.7 million of which sold in China ... Daimler record car sales, up 13% in US to 245,231 and up 31% to 193,339 in China."

What I notice from those indicators is that it is, of course, the middle class who are buying the 1.72 million US$20,000–30,000 Volkswagens and the upper middle who bought the 193,000 $70,000 Benzes. Expressed as a percentage ratio, we have the Volkswagen/Mercedes auto sales ratio in China as an indicator at 8:1 to consider. Multiplying by 100, does this mean China has 172 million middle-class citizens in proportion to 19 million wealthy? It gives us some sense of the demographics here.

If that middle-class population is going to quadruple in a single generation as expected by GS and the UN, we can further extrapolate exponentially increasing car sales numbers and related consumption demand—with car seats for the babies, of course.

Our Man in China Sees No Global Crash (March 2010)

The following essay provoked a firestorm in this forum, so it was run twice. Cavolo's point of view is far more bullish than my own and most of those who responded to it evidently do not share Mario's optimism that the world's financial crisis will simply go away.

—Rick Ackerman

Let's start with a core economic premise and build a scenario of supporting premises as we ponder the new reality of our global economic future without the rhetorical "crash and doomsday" scenarios that almost never play out. Here is the premise to explore: Nothing will crash or collapse. Not the Euro, not the US$, not the stock market of this or that country, and certainly not the entire financial system.

Assets will swing wildly up and down, systems will change, sometimes dramatically, but doomsday collapse is off the table. People who constantly focus on threats of "doomsday this" and "parabolic that" are either too addicted to the emotional thrills attached to such moves, or trying to sell you something. Here we should try to apply a more genuine and balanced analysis of the global economic stage, which is an increasingly complex, fluid, shifting entity.

Now let us build the supporting premises to paint a picture of the new reality in the present and for the next 10 years. The new global reality is a world with unfathomable trillions of sovereign debt over everyone's heads. This is an ongoing reality, a big part of our new reality.

This has been rightfully called a crisis of biblical proportions. However, in this essay, we will just accept it as the new normal reality. We accept it and we adjust to it. Assets will adjust to it. The system will accept it and adjust to it. The value of individual assets will respond to it by swinging up or down 30%–50%, creating significant shifts in society and culture. We can't make it go away, any more than we can change the color of the sky or the rising and setting of the sun.

So, then, applying a little common sense, how will the assets of the world economic system respond to the fact of massive sovereign debt hanging over everyone's heads in the coming years?

Interest Rates

This is easy—yields will eventually go up. Higher and higher debt loads scare lenders, and they will therefore demand higher and higher yields in return. Everybody gets this. *[Author's note: Ben Bernanke's QE1-2-3 has essentially prevented this inevitable interest rate increase for now.]*

This phase of the cycle has begun with Australia, India, China, and the United States during the month of February 2010. Interest rates moving up means stock and bond prices will be moving down. That's why last month Nassim Taleb, author of *Fooled by Random-ness* and *The Black Swan: The Impact of the Highly Improbable,* said everyone should short US Treasury bonds. However, this doesn't mean stocks will "collapse." That's mostly rhetorical nonsense.

We can state there is a very high probability that stocks will not enjoy the bubbles that are normally possible when interest rates are low because people don't want to leave their money in the bank earning next to nothing. When interest rates are rising, people shift their priorities to avoid risk if possible. Why try to earn 15% with the risk of owning stocks if I can leave my money in the bank at 5% with no risk?

Future Is Inflationary

Please don't make the mistake of improperly relating this point to the "failing banks" issue. Yes, we all know there is too much debt and that both sovereign and corporate default on debts is a danger to the financial system. That's a given that the entire system must adjust to. The stock market will not experience a doomsday "collapse" simply because the future is inflationary per the rising-interest-rate scenario that exists. The cost and price of everything will go up, including the price of equity shares. Most agricultural commodities are going up in price for the simple reason of increased global demand from a growing population. More basic stuff.

Stocks may be worth relatively less when measured against some other asset such as gold or dollars, or perhaps Euros or coffee. Just look at a long-term chart of the US stock market and you'll understand the point. When the market declines 30% over a much shorter period of time than it required to go up 50%, many investors want to freak out. But in fact, the market will once again adjust, respond, and start climbing again. It is important to have a sense of the long-term reality of global economics and stock markets. Ignore most of the shorter-term media spin, which has little to do with helping you be wiser and smarter.

Global Currencies

Currencies will continue to devalue. They are in a competitive devaluation game because a lower currency value means cheaper exports to the rest of the world. Right now, the Chinese are in the lead with their refusal to revalue the yuan peg against the dollar. The purchasing power of any currency will continue to decline as it has historically. It is a natural consequence of the global economic order. Due to economic forces on the three major continents, individual currencies will keep dancing up and down 30% against each other. Last year it was US dollar down, euro up; this year, it's euro down, US dollar back up. Anyone can look at a chart and see which way the wind is blowing. The point is that, in the end, the total sum balance of all the currencies added together equals a basket we'll call Basket A, which has the purchasing power to buy a basket of goods and services we'll call Basket B.

Gold

Gold is just another asset to store value, which, in general, keeps going up in value relative to currencies. The part most people miss is the relativity—recently gold went up against the euro, right? No! The euro is going down, so the price of everything, including gold against the euro, is going up priced in euros. To someone holding euros, the price of gold and the price of a vacation in the US are both going up.

Knowing that interest rates are going up long-term and that currencies are devaluing long-term, we can safely assume that gold will also continue going up long-term. It will also go up as it is regarded as a safe-haven asset against government instability and volatility in the global economy. We can see there's plenty of that going around. Your final clue on the floor of the price of gold is that China, India, and George Soros are all buying lots of it at around the current price range of US$1,000–1,100.

Oil and Energy

The price of oil is tricky to get a handle on for a number of reasons. First, the price of oil is highly manipulated and controlled by traders and speculators with billions at their disposal in the futures markets. Meanwhile, the oil industry has become more like a mainstream McDonald's or Nike brand. They are now running a massive, orchestrated "the world needs oil" PR campaign while the world is quite intent on going on a low carbon-fuel diet.

You do know that big corporations, including thee oil giants, retain PR and marketing firms, right? That's not just for crisis response on oil spills. Seems weird, doesn't it? I mean, they're just supposed to be providing a commodity, and what the heck are they doing getting involved in PR and branding? Anyway, the second point about oil is that demand is not going to skyrocket. At best it is going to slowly rise. The third point is that oil production levels are dropping, but again this scenario can change significantly.

The fourth point in the oil discussion is the one we sense the oil industry's PR campaign is trying very hard to downplay in order to postpone a decline in oil prices—that there is now a massive global commitment to developing alternative energy resources. The buildup in this combination of wind, solar, natural gas, and nuclear energy has the potential to put a much more significant dent in the demand for oil than makes them happy.

Of these, nuclear will be most significant because it is already a well-established industry; moreover, due to advances in technology, nuclear safety today has improved multiple generations beyond what it was in the days of Three Mile Island. Over the next few years, as hundreds of new nuclear power plants come online, mostly located in America and China, a complementary pro-nuclear PR campaign will insure that images of nuclear disaster will drift out of the collective psyche. (By the way, my family lived near Three Mile Island the week its reactor had a breach. We high-tailed it to grandma's back in Yonkers for a few weeks!)

Big Oil's Wish

We can sense that big oil wants oil in the US$80–90 range while in reality the price of oil belongs in the US$55–70 range. That would also be much more supportive of the global economy. Finally, the use of alternative energy sources in daily life will cause the routine of our daily lives to change. You will not own a big, fat SUV; you will own an electric car, electric bike, or even electric golf cart–type vehicle that you use only for local trips at 20 mph. You will not buy gas. You will drive home and plug your electric scooter in the wall every 25 miles. You will in fact enjoy the change and appreciate saving money. Electric bikes and scooters have been mainstream transportation in China for years, along with buses and subways. Why do you think Chinese have so much cash? In America, think Sun City where the residents own golf carts to get around the neighborhood. In the future, that lifestyle won't be restricted to retirees.

It is true we are facing global economic circumstances that can be painted with a doomsday brush. We could also use a Chinese silk brush to paint the picture less harshly. If we take the time to look at the situation with long-term eyes and through the eyes of a child, it enables us to understand that whatever is happening in the world of scary global economics, the parts of the system, the various assets in the global economy, adjust and respond in cycles along the way. We must become smarter so that we, too, know how to adjust and respond as effectively as possible, living as we do, here in the new reality.

Bak's Sand Pile

Giving more weight to the more extreme view, I greatly favor Bak's sand pile model as a way of understanding the state we're in. However, when the sand pile randomly breaks and flows downward, its quantity remains the same and it is still sand, ready to be built up again one grain at a time.

As a follow up to the "too optimistic" scenario my article painted, here is my "Four Year Future Forecast." Four years from now:

- The Dow will be close to 14,000 points.
- The value of all real estate in the US, Europe, and China will be the same as current prices, plus or minus 10% at most.
- The yield on the US 30-year treasury bond will reach 6%–7.5% *[Note: Bernanke's QE1-2-3 prevented this.]*
- Gold will be priced US$2,500 an ounce.
- Oil will be priced at US$125 a barrel, with natural gas at US$6 per thousand cubic feet.
- The sticker price of daily goods and services will be marginally higher.
- The US$ and euro indexes against other world currencies will have continued to decline by an additional 30% or more, with two to three wild 25% swings along the way due to "crisis announcements" that will send the world markets reeling.
- The real cost of goods and services will have continued to go up worldwide by an additional 30%, due to the continued decline in the purchasing power of the US$ and euro.
- The Chinese RMB will continue to be controlled by the Chinese government for—practically speaking—eternity. China will, over these next four years, have its expected roller coaster dips, con-

tinue to rise higher and higher in economic global power, yet not open up its country to further internationalization. If anything, they are more likely close their borders than open them any further.

- In the face of higher US Treasury and other bond yields worldwide, pieces of the sovereign debt, pensions, Social Security, and so on will be somehow set aside, forgiven, defaulted, dissolved, off the books, renamed, re-categorized, hidden, reclassified, or adjusted with more market-to-market-type shenanigans; whatever needs to be done, they'll do it.

Doomsday here? No, but it's quietly built in, isn't it? How so? Because currency Basket A will buy less and less value of goods in Basket B, following history. As well pointed out, appreciated, and understood by several comments, the "sovereign debt driven doomsday" is already here; the new reality, built into this scenario, starting geographically at the center of it all, whereby the American Dream of the middle classes has been utterly destroyed, raped, and pillaged. As writer Paul Farrell named the two groups the "Average Joe and Jane" Americans of the world, yet this applies to Europe and China too. The other group is the "Happy Conspiracy" insiders, comprised of two sets: the rotten rich bastards who have heaped this destruction upon us and continue to do so, and the other people who are blessed to be well off, in quality situations, have great careers, and are nice folks.

That's our life on planet Earth in four years: fine for the rich who can weather and profit from the storm, and steadily worse for the "Average Joes and Janes" of the world.

My wife and I want to have our first child this next year. I think with great concern and trepidation, "What is the state of the world we are bringing a child into?"

P.S. On a related note to impending catastrophe—boring, muddling, or otherwise—China is stubbornly refusing to revalue the yuan and the situation has just worsened because now it is a matter of face for them *not* to appreciate it, so you can bet your last fortune cookie they won't. They've just had a surge in imports and exports, but it's still not enough. They'll start raising wages internally to benefit their own country first, which will spur more domestic consumption and more imports. In turn, their concession and rationale to the rest of the world is perfect: "We will continue to buy plenty of US debt, so be nice to us," while giving the West more credit rope to slowly hang itself with. Who's kidding whom about who's in the driver's seat here?

Meanwhile, the inflation here—including the property bubble—is threatening stability. It is going to continue to be cool for the rich and fortunate, but it is going to create misery for the rest of the country; the thing is, this state of affairs may be able to continue along this path for several more years. Reminder to all, once again: consumer debt-to-cash ratio here is still ridiculously low.

His Rosy Outlook Ignores Reality (March 2011)

My response to Mario Cavolo's "rosy" economic outlook kicked off such a spirited discussion in the forum that I am letting it run for a second day. Let me mention, however, that Mario himself has spurned my "optimist" label and said that he sees no roses, only reality. He lays out his case below.

No one doubts that optimists like Mario will be essential when it comes time to rebuild the economy. Might I suggest that you save your energy for later, when it will do the most good, rather than risk squandering even a small amount of it arguing in a forum where you're outnumbered twenty to one? Much creative destruction remains to occur before America can get back on track, and only a great deal of pain can bring about the epiphany that the illusion of our economic well-being has been sustained entirely by lies. (Fortunately, that is not true of our economic future, since Yankee know-how can never be counted out. But merely financing Yankee know-how will require re-allocating capital from a still-vastly overvalued financial sector to one that efficiently turns out real goods and services that the rest of the world vitally needs.

For the present, however, The Great Recession has dealt America's standard of living a mortal blow, steepening our decline in ways that are likely to continue for perhaps a generation. The upper strata of earners has not gotten away unscathed, as you would have us infer, even if the fraudulent, Fed-engineered stock market rally launched exactly two years ago has eased the pain of their dot-com and real estate losses. The stock market must now crash too, since it is buoyed by an all-but-irresistible tide of funny money. Ultimately, however, nearly all classes of assets save bullion, farmland, and a few others are destined for collapse as well, since current valuations are based on a money system whose basic unit of measure is an already worthless dollar. The rentiers and middle-class are not going to escape this inevitable phase of our economic cleansing.

Colleges Selling a Hoax

I don't have the time to refute you, Mario, point-for-point, but to take just one economic "positive" that you've cited—the fact that US colleges are not deserted —is it possible to argue that the colleges are as big a fraud as our money system, channeling more and more undergrads toward worthless graduate degrees (how many more young lawyers, for one, can the system absorb?) because there are presently no jobs for them? You of all people should be acutely aware of this problem, since it is hugely worse for China, where even kids with the engineering degrees that their American counterparts have disdained cannot find jobs in the city above the sweat-shop level. It is not possible to overstate the potentially dire consequences of this for China, especially if exports to the US dry up.

As further regards China, surely they recognize that their US partner is a Ponzi scheme operator—a book-cooking, funny money–printing, lie-peddling swindler who will eventually take them down. Just recently, for instance, following a report in the London Financial Times *that the Federal Reserve had supplanted China as the largest holder of Treasury paper, the US Treasury rejiggered the numbers so that China came out on top. It is disconcerting enough that Treasury can swing these totals by, in this case, more than $200 billion while evidently making it impossible for anyone to ferret out the empirical truth.*

But what makes the adjustment all the more insidious is that it was intended to make the public believe that China has confidence in the US. Bloomberg *news, for one, appears to have*

> *swallowed this load of crap* in toto, *reporting that "China's Treasury holdings underscore the [Chinese] government's confidence in President Barack Obama's stewardship of the economy." Yeah, sure. China, for its part, has not commented on the "adjustment."*
>
> —*Rick Ackerman*

I offer a viewpoint and approach and I can't agree it is optimistic as so suggested but in saying that, I think Rick knows he creates more opportunity for debate here. Indeed I am not an optimist, I am a clarifier and observer of reality and I carefully try not to filter what I see. As the approaches morph, I realize I'm focusing more on the fact of:

America: The Great Schism

That's not the great destruction or doom of all mankind, but a schism; a fresh, wide, ugly, massive, and transforming socioeconomic divide. As when the Protestants had enough of the church's stranglehold, as when the biblical curtain tore, America is today a completely different, transformed, divided entity. Calling this "neo-America" is fine with me; but the neo-America that I refer to is the one defined by the socioeconomic exclusion, marginalization, and ostracism of a sector of its own.

Collectively, the government apparatus and system—big pharma, subsidies, lobbies, banking, insurance, etc.—they are building their own new world. We can say, as Rick has suggested, that the system has already implodded, that they have already pressed the reset button, and they are doing great in their world at the expense of others. They are—that's a fact. How can you tell me that hundreds, even thousands, of companies across the world aren't doing very well, doing business, generating products, services, revenues, and profits? That's delusion too, my friend, because they are obviously doing very well.

Does that mean I am saying there isn't a cost? No. There is certainly an unfortunate cost, which, looked at even closer, reveals mind-boggling greed and illegal activity at the very top of society. Reference the *Rolling Stone* article, "Why Aren't Any of Them in Jail?"*

Can good come from bad? It is God's domain to unravel the mystery; as men we try and fail. Even as we see in front of our face what these high and mighty ***holes are doing, we are impotent to respond in a meaningful way. Here's another way to look at it—yes, it is nuts that a tollgate operator should make US$76,000 per year on an inflated state salary. But is it wrong to be happy for the guy, his wife, and his kids for scoring that? Should we not agree he's lucky? That he can afford to send them to college, to provide better, to be less indebted, all because he was fortunate enough to find a cushy, easy, high-paying job? Doesn't that extra money he makes end up back in the economy being spent?

Or is this just my optimism?

Slave Labor's Last Gasp (June 2010)

From the perspective of Western nations, workers in China and India toil under miserable conditions for slave wages. Things are not quite as bad as that, says Shanghai correspondent Mario Cavolo, and conditions can only continue to improve. In the essay below, drawing on his own experience as a cruise-ship worker, he explains why.

—Rick Ackerman

It is no secret that Europe and America were built on slave labor. As the appalling revelations of the working conditions at Foxconn, Apple's supplier, have recently made clear, China and India are being built on slave labor's modern equivalent. The details of the story vary, but in the end, human beings are working twelve-to-sixteen-hour days, six to seven days per week. They are given a place to sleep at night, a place to occasionally wash, three basic meals per day, and a very low wage, usually the equivalent of US$6 per day. If a worker gets sick, his or her medical expenses are typically paid for. As we continue, however, let's keep thinking about that wage: six dollars a day.

Now let's switch gears and consider the case of a well-established, international industry where people also work like slaves for twelve hours per day, seven days per week. What industry am I referring to? The cruise-ship vacation industry.

During my contract providing entertainment services last year with the Royal Caribbean Cruise line, I realized that despite the harshly long hours and demanding service work, there may seem to be some amazingly attractive travel perks; but while the ship's crew were permitted to disembark for several hours to visit the ports, they were usually too tired and needed to sleep instead, and thus would rarely leave the ship.

Though there is an enormous difference between the type of intense labor demands of cruise-ship workers and that of factory workers in China or India—the largest difference is the monthly wage.

Kitchen crewmembers used to typically be hired from the Philippines or Central America, but with more and more ships sailing Asian waters, many more Chinese are filling these jobs. As part of a cruise ship's hotel operation, they will work, on a contractual basis, twelve to sixteen hours per day, seven days per week for six months, with a six-week rest between contracts and round-trip flight home paid. They are provided a decent shared-cabin bunk, plenty of good food, and full medical coverage. When they are not working, they are sleeping because they are exhausted.

US$180 per Month

However, the typical ship's kitchen or housekeeping crewmember earned around US$1,200 per month or more, paid in cash. For comparison, Chinese and Indian factory workers—such as those involved in the Foxconn factory controversy—were being paid about a fifth of that, or around US$180 per month. With the recent escalation in worker protests and suicides, Foxconn's CEO, who has become a billionaire on the backs of his slaving workers, increased wages by 30%.

Let me ask you this: Does a 30% wage increase remedy the problem? Pretend it is your job: standing for twelve hours, performing a monotonous assembly-line task, during which time you are not allowed to speak to fellow workers. Sounds like the kind of misery that might make some of us think about jumping off a tenth-story ledge. At first blush, it is the low wage that seems intolerable and not the working conditions. But looking more closely at the "low wage" of US$180 per month while considering living costs in China, we find ourselves looking at the equivalent of around US$720 back in the United States.

That is my personal estimate, based on my experience living in China for the last 11 years. And let me mention that recently, I had a terrible headache for which I went to the local hospital and had a CT scan for US$20 (1% the cost of the procedure in the US, where it would generally run about US$2,000). So please believe me when I tell you that the daily cost of living in China reflects typical expenses that are a third to a tenth of those in North America or continental Europe. For instance, a 500 ml bottle of water at the local mart is US$1 or more in the West. Here it's only US$0.20.

Socking It Away

The biggest point of the US$180 wage is that for China factory workers, just like cruise-ship staff, on their off-work hours, they are too tired to spend it. Sleep costs nothing. It is more than obvious to me that the workers' misery lies mainly in their daily working conditions. How does a US$50 monthly raise help my daily misery? They're not spending the US$180 that they are already receiving.

On a cruise ship, the kitchen crew is also working twelve to fifteen hours per day, seven days per week. If they are fortunate, they are moving around from task to task, breaking up the boredom and monotonous routine, rather than say, peeling carrots for twelve hours straight. Then, at the end of the month, the ship's crew is paid relatively generously in cash and benefits. Think about how many typical middle-class American employees can put US$1,000 per month directly in the bank each month after expenses—very few. And so, even though the daily life of a cruise-ship crew is long and tough, and even though their quality of life leaves much to be desired, their progress in real wage earnings—in providing for their families back home, in saving for their future—is clearly meaningful and significant. The savings rate of a cruise ship's crew is typically 70–80%; and be it only US$180 or US$230, the manual laborers in China also save their pay at a similar rate!

So why is China rising? Two key reasons. With the Western economies facing distress and potential disaster in one form or another due to the growing sovereign-debt problem, we easily see that China's private and public sector are far less leveraged. Even if the economy dips, even if the property bubble deflates by 20%–30%, the reaction will be far more muted because 50% to 60% of homeowners in China don't even have mortgages. I am not referring to the 20% who are speculators, but rather to working-class Chinese—a staggering 90% of whom own their own homes*. Based on this, we can assume that 50% of the 1. 36 billion own a home.

Secondly, corporate and state profits are plentiful, with hundreds of millions of lower- and middle-class employees taking home slave wages. The country's infrastructure is being magnificently and broadly built out. Combine these two factors and you begin to see the current window in which China and, similarly, India, are able to make rapid economic progress and increase their economic power. As occurred long ago in the Western economies, over the coming years, the economic evolution of societies that are modernizing will be inflationary, with steadily rising wages and better working conditions contributing to a rising standard of living. As in Europe and America, slave labor in China and India will soon be brought to an end through the power of economic development alone.

Risk of Depression Low Says Our Man in China (July 2010)

We frequently run guest commentaries expressing opinions that differ markedly from our own. Below, Mario Cavolo, an expatriate who lives in China, argues that there is no global, deflationary depression bearing down on us, but rather a muddle-along economy with strong spots as well as weak ones. We disagree and see a period of economic darkness more severe and widespread than any ever recorded.

This is because the world is unwinding a financial asset bubble with a notional value of nearly a quadrillion (i.e., $1,000,000,000,000,000) dollars. Considering the sum involved, there can be no easy or quick return to economic health. More logical is that a totally corrupt global financial system will have to be destroyed before we can rebuild the economy on honest trade. As things stand, the world's financial-products-and-services balance sheet is at least ten times as large as the ledger for trade in real goods and services.

Mario notes optimistically that Japan has muddled through its decades-long deflationary recession without experiencing social disintegration. Although this is true, we would argue that it is so only because Japan had the rest of the world—including an insatiable US consumer—to keep its powerful export machinery humming as it traversed deflation's valley of death. But who will bail out the US and Europe as we continue to sink together?

—Rick Ackerman

China's Huge Home Equity

I think the depression is not as bad as it seems in the West, but let's focus on China and do a little calculation supporting my realization that while things might be tight in the West, China will do just fine and have a major role in keeping the rest of us afloat; I've said the rich are richer than ever here, with the rising middle class of 300 million also richer than ever, rising proudly and happily. To give you an example, let's look at just one key slice of the Chinese population with the following conservative calculation: there are around 100 million homeowners with equity in their homes that has increased from US$50,000 to US$150,000 over the past decade and a half, an equity value totaling $15,000,000, 000,000.

That's fifteen trillion in home equity wealth with no mortgages—and that's on top of rapidly rising salaries. In the cycle of economic rises and declines, it's China's time to rise—with both the upper and middle classes taking the spoils. Good for them, as they are as entitled as any other nation-state to prosper and grow, and now is their time.

So here we reach our happy conclusion: there is plenty in the pockets of the combined army of rich and new semi-rich in the US, Europe, and China to sustain the economic status quo and avoid a collapse. Will the bubble burst in the face of this asset-inflation-created wealth? Nonsense, and I'm tired of hearing it. What bubble? Which bubble? This kind of talk is becoming both misleading and self-serving disinformation fed to the masses via the complicit media. In America and Europe, the rich are richer than ever. In China, the rich and middle class are rising and richer than ever. That's not a formula for the collapse of anything.

Keynesian Rape

However, it is a setup for the continuation of the Keynesian raping of the world, which is being arranged by those in power to simply absorb the entire mess via continued price inflation and decline of currency purchasing power; the only exception being US real estate and wages, more than offset by the polar opposite happening in China!

What will happen—and what is happening—is this: One slice of the asset pie at a time, in some bizarrely rhythmic fashion, will continue to inflate. For example, Chinese wages and prices are inflating and will continue to do so for years to come. Real estate will flatten a bit but, with little leverage, any sharp property value declines will be quickly absorbed and forgotten. Just think of the US expansion starting from the '60s and you can easily see the point. Then another couple of slices also inflating globally—crude oil and gold for example. Up, up, up they will go. The cost of energy and water supply: heading up. But not US middle-class wages and real estate. Those are two slices of the pie not likely to budge anytime soon. But that's only two slices of a very large and complex pie.

Conclusions

The final conclusion is twofold. First, that the richer and richer hundreds of millions in the global economy that we identified in this article will sustain the global economy and are easily able to absorb the continued world-wide inflation of prices and decline in currency purchasing power. They will still sleep soundly at night. Interest rates, by the way, must remain low relative to risk or these folks will stop spending and investing in the asset classes.

Bonds won't collapse because instead currencies will simply decline in purchasing power across the global board. The daily purchasing power of "the haves" will of course also deteriorate along with everyone else's, but so what? They will "cut back" but still buy extra virgin olive oil, brand name clothes, send their kiddies to a good college, and go to the IMAX if they feel like it because they can afford it. Their lives will remain relatively protected, nice and comfortable. Secondly, The rest of the world, starting with the struggling middle class on down, will feel poorer and poorer over the coming years—a daily reality much easier to deal with if you live in China or elsewhere in Asia than if you live in the US or Europe.

One might ask if there is a historic migration from a declining US to somewhere else in the cards? Maybe, but don't think for a moment that there's going to be a welcoming "Ellis Island" anywhere near Chinese shores.

It is easy to continue feeling humbled and confused by the sentimental and fundamental dance of the world's asset classes and regions, be they equities, currencies, commodities, or that shiny stuff; feel free to pick your basket of market sectors to analyze and track.

Planet Hollywood was a great brand name idea. Today, so is Planet Las Vegas or Planet Macau. The singular "George Soros who made billions shorting the British pound" example has become a cancerous plurality on the daily tape in a high-stakes global trading playground. It is indeed real, a separate "sector" of reality, while the rest of reality—the real reality of the real world—goes on day by day, dealing with the damage trickling down.

The One Exception

The rich are richer than ever the world over, and there's more than enough evidence available to confirm that this is the case. Furthermore, this is on such an unprecedented global scale now that China and her citizens have led the rise of the APAC region to prominence and power alongside the American and European economic blocs. As we shall see, America's decline is the decline of only one main sector of her economy, along with the rise of others.

No, the baby is not going to be thrown out with the global bath water, and there will be no doomsday collapse with one exception: a 30% chunk of the middle class in America whose lives and careers and futures have been decimated. They may as well pack their bags and come to the APAC/China region to teach English at 20 bucks an hour, because that's loads better than anything they are going to find staying put. Those are the folks in the wrong place at the wrong time in the annals of history's economic and political cycles. We should genuinely feel for their plight, including many whom I know personally.

Inflationary Vortex to Hell?

What does it all mean? Let's make sure we understand where the balance points lie and have a clear understanding of what to expect in the coming years. Rick and a number of his loyal, fabulously intelligent and respecting followers make a well thought-out case for an impending, downward spiral into hell, which, however, will simply never occur.

Until you can wrap your mind around the idea of being sucked downward into a spiraling vortex that is simultaneously being sucked upward into an inflationary vortex, you're missing today's and tomorrow's reality. We have quite the dichotomy to resolve, and it is not a question of inflation vs. deflation. It will not only go one way or the other. Different regions and sectors of the now intricately connected global economy will experience vastly different economic impacts.

Oh, joyful global happy days for so many more than ever before! Do you know that? That's a fact to contend with, not argue about, making it very hard to reconcile with predictions of a worldwide doomy, gloomy deflation scenario. We've talked about how the Japanese economy spent fifteen years in deflationary hell, going nowhere. But if the majority of her citizens had a million in the bank and a house worth that much, who really cared? In the end, if the trappings of daily life are comfortable, if you know your home is secure, you have enough money to make it to your death and beyond, what's the fuss if the economy sucks?

This lack of economic stress is typical of the mindset of today's newly rich Chinese citizen, and her poor citizens and newly rich middle-class citizens as well. While it may be frustrating and annoying, it is not a big problem to be unemployed if you have US$200,000 in the bank and a home worth US$300,000 with no mortgage, like most of your neighbors.

Better to Be Poor or Rich in China

Let's get the "poor in China" debate out of the way quickly. If you're poor in the US, you're really screwed from several points of view. If you're poor in China, you're not. Life can still be very safe and comfortable as you can easily rent a decent apartment at only US$200 a month, half that with a roommate. Why? Because you don't need a car to get a low-paying job, your expenses at the level of "local" life are a fifth to a tenth those you'd face in America; you can rent a comfortable room for US$75 (the room I rented in Huntington Beach back in the early '90s was US$450 per month) and there are no minority drug gangs with guns around destroying the neighborhood and threatening your safety—that's even true today in magnificent Shanghai!

You can eat three, square, freshly cooked meals of steamed meat and vegetable buns, noodles, or rice, with veggies and a protein for US$5 total. You can ride an old bicycle no one will steal, and which can be replaced for US$10 if it is stolen anyway. Your medical expenses are equally cheap, starting with antibiotics for US$3 (cipro or cefradine, for example) when you catch a winter cough and fever. You can even get a body massage with a haircut and a happy ending for less than US$20, for those of you who understand what I just wrote. It's hard to imagine such a daily lifestyle, eh?

Yes, it is accessible and normal to a person who is struggling to get on their feet here in China, making it a fabulous place to be "poor." And let's take a final moment for the supposedly miserable 800 million farmers; they have plenty of food, they live in brick dwellings with cheap coal-brick oil barrels to stay warm in winter, they eat three square meals a day, freshly picked and cooked. I'm not saying it's great. They toil the fields twelve hours a day, but it's just basic countryside living and I wouldn't call that "poor" as a typical Westerner defines poor or poverty in urban areas. This by no means implies I am pro-China or think China will save the world, but we need to recognize that the country is a new "third" enormous source of wealth, which has been recently added to the global economy. It only serves as a supporting reference to the point of the article, that there is a larger-than-ever global constituency of upper- and middle-class wealthy who will keep the world's economy muddling along. How dare one suggest a modicum of stability rather than instability?

This brings us back to the core concern of Rick's site, which is that this article assumes there even is a global economy to muddle along in the first place.

We share the fear that at the hands of certain governments and power-mongers to be feared, that we will end up with a worldwide "Argentina" or "Finland." As I've read many times, a scenario of hyperinflation/massive currency devaluation is only caused by a root government policy decision. Barring that, the world's currencies will continue to devalue in relative buying power, slowly choking those who have not accumulated enough assets to live comfortably.

Yes, we are at the mercy of the madmen in charge. Just remember that the goal of those in charge in China is national stability and continued improvement of the entire society based on a series of well-defined Five Year Plans, which they have clearly accomplished on an unprecedented scale. Without question, that is their goal and approach, so if you think otherwise and have some unfounded bias about the "horrible Chinese Communists," you are sorely mistaken. Another thing to keep in mind is that ultimately their interest is for their own country to maintain its position as the center of the earth, far from the defined ideals of what the word "America" originally meant, a place where anyone could come and be free. China has no such internationalist agenda, no warm and fuzzy idealism in its ways of running the country. They're pure pragmatists.

On the other hand, while I don't get the sense that national stability and the good of the citizens and country is the goal of the madmen in charge in the US, it is unfortunately still the lone superpower of the world. It cannot be denied that this scenario does put us all at quite a risk of a serious destabilization. This article does recognize that many will be on the receiving end of bad tidings as the many complex balances of global life and economics continue to shift.

The key sub-theme driving my approach and belief is that the global interconnectedness we experience today is unprecedented: Beyond comprehension, beyond complexity, and beyond deleveraging. (This is addressed in Ramo's book *The Age of the Unthinkable*). Therefore, it is incorrect to suggest that a single currency such as the US$ or euro will be decimated, or to look at the past to suggest possible future outcomes. It hardly matters at all anymore that we can say "the US did this with their currency. "

I am officially discounting Taleb's "black swan" event. There is no such animal. The depth of sector interconnectedness trumps all. It is the new global glue. The whole basket can't collapse together, it is impossible in the interconnected global reality of today. If some wild black swan goes flying up or down (you name your crisis here . . .) something else on the other side of the markets, the other side of the Goldman Sachs trading desk, will go up.

Say US equities start tanking; we'll just rotate to Chinese equities, European equities, currencies, oil, or gold for a few months. Is this the end of the US as we know it? Hardly.

One year after this, when all we rotated into is the new overbought and US equities are now oversold, then we're back into US equities! Everyone has gotten way too smart, therefore canceling out how smart they are. Capitalism, in the free market, has trumped what is best for a country and its citizens. The quality of life of the average citizens will be the price in this new world order, which has already arrived.

Per respected investment guru Charles Nenner, there will be 40% price swings on many securities, so be ready; but per Mario, there will be no doomsday collapse.

Now, let's move toward the validity of the key opposing point to this article, which is no small thing: that the US government has destroyed the future of the world by printing trillions of unnecessary dollars. Skipping the analyses we've all read, it's obvious the whole thing can't possibly have a reasonable winding down or solution. Given this, let's imagine that instead of just accusations, we definitively know that the key government leaders and neo-elitist power-mongers of the world had a real roundtable meeting at which they simply agreed to take this course of action. Something like, "Okay, we want to get richer and richer and need to get more and more control of our countries and no matter what, we know that the little guy is going to suffer, but we can't change that anyway. Let's respond to the current set of crises by printing trillions of US dollars. It will mess up the system, but we will be in position to hoard more, and so relative to the currency devaluations that will result worldwide, we'll be on top to rebuild the future once again. "

Something like that seems to be what's going on, in which case, the three key points I have put forth in this article are very reasonable to expect. So what is actually going to happen in the next few years?

- Major currencies will all go down in value and purchasing power, they will suffer together because of the excess printing of US$, though the gory details unfolding across global markets we can only guess at. (*Note: the world's sovereign banks have now joined the US in issuing hundreds of billions in bonds.*)
- The rich and the almost rich will be relatively okay no matter what, because they are relatively unleveraged. My point here is the size of this group is much larger than is commonly thought.
- The rest will experience decline and in fact will become wards of a deeper and deeper socialism in the US and across the globe. That's not such an unusual idea to Europe and Asia, but it's very new and disruptive to the US. Nevertheless, the transformation has arrived and is accelerating.

The Fifteen Trillion Dollar Home Equity Question (January 2010)

We proffer the always-sunny thoughts of Mario Cavolo, an expatriate who lives in China. His very bullish outlook for the global economy contrasts with some of the gloomier think-pieces that have appeared in this space. In the essay below, Mario extrapolates a very positive economic outcome from the US$15 trillion of unencumbered equity that Chinese property owners currently have vested in their homes. Will the eventual leveraging of this still debt-free sum, together with the irresistible power of China's growing economy, be sufficient to pull the world out of its funk? Read on for Mario's optimistic answer.

—Rick Ackerman

Current United States mortgage debt? US$15 trillion.

Current China home equity? US$15 trillion.

Mortgage debt on those homes? [Close to] Zero.

It is easy to suggest that this insight, which reveals a US$30 trillion spread between US home mortgage debt and Chinese home equity, better enables us to grasp the underlying forces impacting the economic power shift we are seeing from West to East. While it might be in vogue these days to criticize the US for being built on a mountain of debt, I'd rather not. Let's first take a moment to remember the positive effect the world over that the judicious and reasonable use of debt has had over the past 50 years; that very same debt-based financial system enabled the United States to become, by an enormous margin, the largest economy in the world while the rest of the world's countries also enjoyed their own growth riding on the American red, white, and blue coattails.

In truth, that never would have happened without the US debt-financing binge, so let's not pretend otherwise. Countries love to complain about America's debt but they've enjoyed riding along as she rose these past five decades. The economic power of Japan and China lag far behind at only US$4 trillion each, followed by Germany in the US$3 trillion range. Maybe if they had committed to more debt to build industry and consumption, they'd also have proportionately higher GDP.

Alas, we note with grave concern that the words "judicious and reasonable" have been removed from the debt-usage formula in recent years, but that is not our focus here. While China, at the government banking level, has also done more than its fair share of economic stimulus lending these past few years, Chinese homeowners stand alone as a large piece of the world's economic puzzle, with trillions in fresh, new home equity that will eventually make its way into the Chinese and global economies. There are 150 million lower- and middle-class homes in China now worth an average of US$100,000 each, and few of them have mortgages.

That's US$15 trillion in home equity that has yet to be borrowed from and injected into the consumer economy. In contrast, US mortgage debt is also US$15 trillion and many homeowners owe more than their home is worth.

China's Equity Miracle

Let's argue for a moment that the US mortgage and China equity numbers we started with may be too general or generous to be meaningful. However, digging deeper into the history of property appreciation in the US and China, that argument falls flat fairly quickly for an amazing reason: a key economic growth curve that took 40 years to create in the US took only ten years in China. Hence, what looks like an economic miracle is really no more than an even course upward with no direct end in sight.

We recall that US suburban home prices back in the 1960s were in the range US$30,000–60,000. Those millions of homes today fall in a price range of US$90,000–250,000. A time span of over 40 years was required to achieve that level of appreciation in value—a long, slow appreciation curve. Can we confirm that average home equity is perhaps 20% today? Yes, we can. Thirty percent of homeowners in the US have no mortgages. The other homes in aggregate with mortgages barely have a dime of equity.

Now let's take a look at China's home property value appreciation curve. The unprecedentedly steep curve in China's economic expansion explains a large proportion of the rising shift in economic power toward China. US$15 trillion of home equity with no mortgage debt sheds even more light on the new reality. What would the US be like if 50% of households were freed of their mortgage payments?

Comparing Home Values

Back in 2001, China's first-tier cities such as Shanghai and Beijing had similar local apartment prices as in the 1960s US, in the range of US$30,000–60,000. Home values in the mainstream second-tier cities such as Dalian, Shenyang, Tianjin, and Chengdu, were lower by half again, more like US$15,000–30,000, equaling US$40–75 per square foot.

There are no mortgages on any of those millions of apartments. Did you know that home mortgages hardly even existed in China in 2000 and they probably didn't even have Chinese words back then for the term "credit card?" Only ten years later, property in the media-worn first-tier "property bubble" cities have increased in value an average seven-fold, from US$30,000–60,000 to US$200,000–400,000, while in second-tier cities, property prices have increased a much more reasonable four-fold, from US$15,000–30,000 to US$60,000–120,000 across a much wider swath of the Chinese population. Considering normal long-term global economic cycles and property values, US$60,000–120,000 is a range those millions of households are likely to never decline below again.

School Teacher Example

Let me give you an accurate example to illustrate; a typical Chinese retired schoolteacher living in her five-story walk-up, 80-square-meter apartment, located in a garden apartment complex of 800 similar apartments in which we find all of the area's retired schoolteachers living on pensions of US$300 per month with medical coverage.

During their career well over 15 years ago, they were allowed to purchase this apartment for RMB 800 per square meter, which at that time was about US$10 per square foot. Today, the apartments are worth five times that: RMB 4,000 per square meter, or US$50 per square foot, which equals close to US$60,000, still a relatively modest valuation. The new apartment developments in the surrounding neighborhood are certainly much nicer and valued at closer to US$100,000, which makes sense and is still within a reasonable range for urban middle-class home prices.

Why? Because the city in general has been rebuilt and revitalized; because a new 180-kilometer-an-hour subway line is going in with a stop just ten minutes' walk away; because Sheraton, Marriott, Hong Kong New World Towers, Kerry Center, and Shangri-La hotels have all appeared around the new convention center area downtown; and because several multinational companies have set up shop in or outside the city, cranking out cars, car parts, software, and medical equipment.

Needless to say, these 800 retired schoolteacher home-owners all have 100% equity in their homes. That equity will eventually make its way into the economy. Even within 10 years, many of these elderly will pass away, leaving the asset to their children who will most likely sell it and use the money in some other way, adding money to the economy. As they increase their tendency to borrow against this asset, that will add even higher levels of domestic consumption, a trend we take a closer look at further on.

The Scottsdale Home

Back in the US, the Scottsdale, Arizona, home I sold in 1995 for US$110,000 is still valued at US$180,000 today, even after a 30%

drop from its peak value a couple of years back. With the US economy still struggling, many expect that property values will still fall further. Understand that, on the other hand, China is on the classic inflationary rise—including all the historical hallmarks one finds in such a situation, such as rising prices and rising wages, supported not only by the popular reasons most often cited in the media, but also by the economic foundation of this unprecedented mortgage-free equity pool.

Does a fresh pool of 70 million mortgage-free homes scattered across dozens of China's second-tier cities valued today at US$60,000–120,000 plus an additional 30 million homes valued at US$200,000–400,000 pack an economic punch strong enough to at least blunt the world's economic woes? To answer that question, there are a couple of related variables to consider, one of which is that Chinese are still loath to borrow on their home equity.

When you buy something in China, you pay cash or you don't buy it. However, we can consider entrepreneurial business owners as more likely to borrow—and who may borrow up to 70% of their home equity from a bank to build their businesses. We find that even borrowing of this nature is not yet a widespread practice in China. If the home equity loan rate hit 30% of equity, that would conceivably add US$3–5 trillion of spending to the Chinese economy in the coming years, a welcome addition as far as the Chinese government is concerned to help stimulate domestic consumption.

Related to the question of such trends in lending and borrowing, Chinese today are still the world's greatest savers, with a 30%-plus savings rate. As Chinese consumers start borrowing more on their massive home equity pool to consume and make entrepreneurial investments, they will have additional monthly loan payments and the national savings rate could perhaps come down to 20%.

Even a 20% savings rate would still be regarded as amongst the highest savings rates in the world compared to other countries. So when trying to understand the many factors that are supporting China's rise, bear in mind the powerful factors we have discussed here, like this enormous home-equity pool, which stands quietly in the shadows as a leg of support behind the more popular topics and analysis of China in the media.

One key point is that the US needs to seriously evaluate where it is in the global economy. If you visit the website of the American Chamber of Commerce in Shanghai (amcham-shanghai.org), you will find an article by Chairman Robert Roche that shows that the Chamber, which is, of course, in support of US businesses, is encouraging the National Export Initiative. Indeed! The US is getting its butt kicked and it better start thinking about the fundamental realities of producing and exporting whatever else it is the rest of the world, which is getting richer by the day, might want to buy from her. (Note: Since this was written the US has gotten the message as exports to China are steadily and substantially rising to record levels. Expect this to continue.)

I'll remain respectfully provocative—no doom, no crash. Let's be reasonable here. Every single time the market does anything but go up, the world seems to forget that even a 10–15% correction would be a reasonable expectation. What, the stock market is currently outrageously overvalued? It isn't.

Rick clearly knows we are broke and offers brilliant, insightful analysis. But why does it have to be so complicated or disastrous? Yes, we are indeed broke, incredibly broke with a system that is rotten to the core and yet to experience the next set of rollercoaster shenanigans triggered by some next financial or societal apocalyptic black swan.

Fine—but so what? This will all be reflected in four simple trends:

- The continuing decline in the value of currencies, starting with the US$. Nothing new there.
- Inflation—the price of stuff just continues to increase. Nothing new there, either.
- Lower- and middle-class lifestyles and opportunities in further decline. Still nothing new.
- Rich folks' lifestyles better than ever. When hasn't this been the case?

Lots of people getting screwed along the way?

Yep, that's not new.

The country's values and the integrity of the system gone to hell? Yep, that's not new either and the calls to string up the greedy bureaucrats responsible for this mess are certainly warranted.

What can any one of us do about it except adjust our own lives accordingly? This might even mean doing what we can to "exit" this matrix. Myself and hundreds of thousands of expats living overseas have certainly done that to some degree, already residing for many years as locals overseas. But there are plenty of plusses and minuses to bear with that choice, and it isn't for everybody.

Meanwhile, one might dare to say Bernanke is brilliant, doing the only thing he knows he can do in response to the Chinese who stubbornly refuse to let their RMB float and appreciate to where it "should" be in the global currency playing field. So we'll devalue the dollar and a few years later when US assets are more attractively priced, the money and investment and growth will start to flow back in.

It wouldn't be an unreasonable strategy, if it weren't for so much damn damage along the way.

Can China's Miracle Keep the West Afloat? (August 2010)

The response to Mario Cavolo's glowing take on China and the global economy was eye-opening, to say the least. It's not hard to understand why someone who lives and works in China, as Mario does, might believe that the country's economic prospects are so spectacular as to all but preclude the possibility of a deflationary depression elsewhere in the world. We're not so sure ourselves and have a few things to say about it below. But we were nonetheless persuaded by Mario's argument, and by comments made by others in this forum that Mario's case is worth examining.

—Rick Ackerman

Chinese Solutions

Nearly everyone I know in China is acutely aware of the various problems that China faces. They are, however, adamant that they are Chinese problems for which they will find Chinese solutions. Many of my Chinese acquaintances indicate that export trade continues to be quite strong but significantly more of it is going to other emerging markets in the Middle East, Russia, South Africa, South America, and of course, Asia. There is a growing conviction that future export growth will be generated by hi-tech and value-added products.

The Chinese are moving out into the world. They are using their cash to acquire assets everywhere, particularly oil and minerals. They are gaining export markets in developing countries and are becoming major tourists (who are now known to spend more than tourists from any other country). They acknowledge the somewhat symbiotic relationship that they have with the US and Europe and are sufficiently pragmatic to take actions that support those economies.

In the final analysis, China will do what it perceives is best for China. If the West derives a benefit, then so be it.

America's Suicide

> *The burgeoning deficits and the resulting tax burden that results will kill any remote chance the US economy had of recovering, in our opinion.*
>
> *In his essay, Mario asserted that America's fall will be softened by the countervailing pressure of Asian prosperity and by growth elsewhere in the world. He also thinks the super-rich will escape misfortune simply by moving their money out of the US. We would argue that this gives the supposed "smart money" more credit than it deserves.*
>
> *Consider, for one, that whenever some urgent change in investor perceptions scares the allegedly smart money into fleeing one supposed safe haven for another, the smart money will be subject to an enormous haircut. Just ask Warren Buffett, who has been struggling to unwind a US$5 billion position in muni bonds before the music stops.*
>
> *And besides Buffett, there have been many thousands of super-rich investors who have been decimated because they jumped into private-equity deals that they thought were bargains, only to discover that deflation has barely begun to mark down the assets they'd acquired. (Newspaper publishing companies have become the new Brooklyn Bridge that someone would love to sell you.) There is no such thing as a buy-and-hold investment anymore and no asset class is safe from the ravages of capital flight. For that reason, even George Soros can lose a big piece of his net worth if he guesses wrong just once, or if he is just a few hours late exiting a speculative position that has turned lethal.*
>
> —*Rick Ackerman*

Speaking of Soros . . .

> *Speaking of Soros, he supposedly is in Petrobras up to his eyeballs. But does he hold US treasuries as well, as many well-heeled investors undoubtedly do? If so, how smart is that? The US is bankrupt and has been raising its current, US$13 trillion debt ceiling at the rate of US$1 trillion per year. When the epiphany of US bankruptcy finally comes, as it one day must, and the Federal Reserve becomes the only buyer of Treasury paper, where will the smart money (i.e., the hedges) migrate? And how much time will they have to do so? It is hardly beyond conjecture that the inevitable collapse of the dollar and Treasury debt will occur in mere hours, making it impossible for any of the rats to escape the ship.*
>
> —*Rick Ackerman*

Harmonious Society

Right now, creating a harmonious society is China's top priority and value. At his annual presentation for the American Chamber in Shanghai, titled "Marketing to China's Seniors," Tom Doctoroff, Greater China CEO for JWT and author of *Billions: Selling to the New Chinese Consumer*, reminded the audience that the overriding value and priority for the Chinese government and society is to produce a "harmonious society" and for individuals to live and contribute well within their harmonious society. From what I can see, this is being achieved.

Secondly, modern China has always had—and continues to follow—a series of "five-year plans." They define and execute these plans quickly and practically.

But now for the paradox, the "bad side" Rick points out. They will not allow any individual to threaten that "harmonious society." Your rights to do and say what you wish are lower than the rights and needs of the society within which you live. Make no mistake, daily life here is perfectly normal and better than ever, but you must toe the line and do not have the freedom to say and do as you wish politically.

I will not write and post a piece in my blog that criticizes the Chinese government, or criticize the government in public venues such as Am-

Cham events or when I am asked to give a keynote at a conference. I, and others, would never publicly say anything more than "Yes, it is known that this issue has been raised ... and we are concerned about ..." if asked. We would never publicly criticize our hosts or their plans. We do not have that particular freedom here. Like Singapore, don't throw your chewing gum on the ground; they mean it and that's the way it is.

More to the point: No, China's miracle alone cannot keep the West afloat. In the recent article that Rick has published, I put forth the point that the combined total of the rich and almost rich in the US and Europe plus the rich and newly rising rich in China are a total global combined sector of greater strength and power than most give credit, and which could keep the global ship from a complete "Titanic" event.

At the same time, make no mistake there are other global sectors in genuine decline, primarily the American (and European) middle and lower-middle classes. In the immediately previous decades, they had opportunities available to them to improve their lot in life and, indeed, they rose up. In today's new reality, they simply have far fewer such opportunities, while the tide has turned in the economic favor of China, much as it did for the US 50 years ago.

Thus, the doomsday scenario is reduced to the possibility of a specific political action or set of actions decided at the global government level, known in advance by those decision makers, that their decision will be a severe currency revaluation or result in one, in which case, yes, there it is in our faces.

So whilst waiting for that day of sudden and swift transformation as several have suggested here, all is fairly well in the current balance of global affairs, isn't it? In this particular decade on planet Earth, 100 million people in particular have happily risen, while another 100 million people have seen their standard of living decline. Whether we happen to like the country that those people are citizens of is not the point, is it? A "doomsday" means someone somewhere is going to finally, as I remember someone on this forum saying, "hit the reset button" as the unavoidable way of dealing with the excess debt issue.

While this could happen, until then, let's clearly and truly know the current reality we live in from macro to micro, and respond accordingly in our circumstances as best we can. I put forth that a more gradual, quietly miserable inflation and deflation of currency purchasing power is how the excess debt problem will unravel, rather than a cataclysmic type of financial disaster event. How I expect this will unfold:

- Continued price inflation and decline of currency purchasing power; the only exception being US real estate and wages.
- Crude oil and gold will continue to go up, up, up. (Note: the discovery of vast oil and gas reserves accessible via fracking technology may thankfully help keep crude oil prices down for the foreseeable future while also being a key factor in supporting the US economy and jobs problem. The cost of energy and the water supply: heading up. But not US middle-class wages and real estate valuations. Those are two slices of the pie not likely to budge anytime soon. But those are only two slices of a very large and complex pie.)
- The rest of the world, starting with the struggling middle class on down, will feel poorer and poorer over the coming years, a daily reality much easier to deal with if you live in China or Asia than if you live in the US or Europe.

It's actually not a rosy picture painted, but far less severe than a "day of reckoning" type scenario. Certainly none of us wants to wake up to that newscast.

Our "Sci-Fi" Economic Future

While China has seen incredible problems, why should we reach back to dark years past? My mother-in-law was sent to the countryside and had a rough life. I understand, but that's all past here, my friend. The US became the US because we slaughtered the Indians. We all have our shadows to deal with.

- There have been failed construction projects among the US$15 trillion in new real estate wealth that has been created . . . so?

- Yes, there is plenty of corruption . . . what country doesn't have it?
- Yes, business can be ruthless here . . . is this different from anywhere else?
- Yes, private companies have done bad things, like use melamine in milk products, and factories set up "clean room" standards and don't follow them because the local owner and managers don't care . . . but enforcement of standards was far more lax and continues to improve dramatically.

The factory owners responsible for such acts, when caught, are often executed for threatening the public good, for threatening to ruin people's lives. Does that make sense to you?

Yes, prisoners, people who hurt other people are treated quite badly, with fewer rights and greater disdain, and are led out the back door to be executed more often that in the US . . . but I would righteously kill the man who raped my child, cause him untold pain, and I would have no regret at the pearly gates for having done so. Wouldn't you? Are we really so different?

I've watched this scene many times: When a local street thief is caught in China, the local men surround him taunt him, slap him around, treat him like the dog he is; it's crude, it's raw, it's real, and they feel that it's gratifying to give him what he deserves as he dared to threaten their lives and their families. A few minutes later the police show up and they watch for a while, mainly just to make sure no one hits him too hard. Then they take him to jail. Typically he'll spend a month to a year doing hard labor and be released.

Wouldn't you like it if you saw a local drug gang, who ruined an entire neighborhood, being treated that way in America? Wouldn't you cheer? So what's better in this case, the American way or the Chinese way? Every country and every situation has its good and its bad as we might judge it.

On a different front, how can anyone think we're in a time that resembles the prerequisite market sentiment and technical factors that precede a crash? We have no blow-off top, we have no giddy woo-haa, we have no extreme bullishness; what we do have is loads of cash on the sidelines, a great deal of fear, and the wall of worry is as here right now as it has ever been. I could go on; suffice it to say, the pieces of the puzzle are just not there, plus the rules of the system are not the same.

Yes, a news report of a crushing black swan event that may then lead to cascading damages in the economic framework of the world could occur and equities will certainly be part of that along with everything else in the system. But to trade and invest anticipating that possible event is absurd. Until then, as is known and done with the guidance and advisory of sites like this one, intelligent swing and day trading is possible, though difficult.

Support in the 9,500 range should continue to hold, and remember that the markets barely moved, stuck in the 10,000–11,000 range, from 2004 to 2006. Barring some kind of disruptive event, we could see a similar period of stagnation again. Nothing says the markets have to move beyond a certain trading range, and in the low interest-rate environment that is likely to persist for the near future, that is exactly what they may do.

It is of limited help to compare the coincidence of historical charts and circumstances because the circumstances have shifted beyond most of our ability to comprehend. Numbers in trillions? Most people can't grasp the idea of 100 million or 5 billion or 300 billion, let alone trillions. Instant global interconnectedness? It's still beyond our understanding. Joshua Ramo visits the matter nicely in his book *The Age of the Unthinkable*, where all the old rules simply don't work or apply any more. Nothing responds as expected anymore, economically or politically, with the new instant interconnectedness of both systems and knowledge (such as a media landscape where CNN is faster than the CIA at gathering intelligence) on a broad global scale.

As mentioned, we now have zillions of "I'm finally as smart as the Wall Street guys" traders shorting the market. But as soon as the game is discovered, that rule no longer applies! The big guys routinely run the stops. A friend of mine once used the phrase "a guppy in a shark's tank" referring to men dealing with women, but it applies even better here.

It in was a Todd Harrison article* where I read computers running HFT algorithms now make up 70% of trading volume.

It is 2010. The sci-fi cyborg economic future has already arrived. The Wall Street stock market should now be more regarded as a privately run organization managed by a not-officially-recognized yet very real body of government, institutional, and bank elites; a market trading system that also still allows public participants to join in at their ignorant peril or success, if properly armed.

Asian Money Will Eventually Revive the US (March 2011)

The commentary that follows elicited a deluge of fascinating responses, and so it ran for two days. Frequent contributors to the Rick's Picks *forum were asked where the US economy would be in five years. Below, Mario Cavolo, an expatriate whose business is based in Shanghai, says Chinese wealth is clamoring for bargains in the US and that a falling dollar will bring enormous Asian investment to our shores, infusing the US economy with new vitality. The bad news is that large swaths of the American middle class will be devastated by the shifting economic landscape, unable to take advantage of the opportunities that voracious demand from foreigners will create.*

—Rick Ackerman

There are far too many complex pieces to the puzzle across not only America but the entire global market, so intricately interconnected, making it foolhardy to suggest their status or direction.

I would suggest we can agree on a few core points giving us a sense of where we will be in five years, and with that in mind, let's say we have some very good news and some very bad news. No matter how many points we cover, there will be dozens of other points and counterpoints not touched, requiring a 600-page book to cover it all respectably. Yet, with regard to the core points put forth in this treatment, each of us needs to consider what possible moves, what choices, what adjustments he or she might make looking forward to his or her future from today—not as a person who happens to live in a certain state in the United States, but as a person who lives on planet Earth.

The Very Good News

Five years from now, the year 2016 will mark the beginning of America's recovery. That is very good news. All countries go through long-term economic cycles that must be respected. Make no mistake, the US, with all of her problems, with all of her incompetent, greedy, irresponsible, elite leaders, with all of her deeply flawed banking and trading practices, is still a powerhouse—it is still by far the world's largest economy, a resilient and dynamic force in the world politically, economically, and militarily. Add it up. Rome will not burn while Nero fiddles. Rome will transform, Rome will reshape, Rome will respond. Rome will never stop being Rome. Rome will always be a powerhouse on the global economic and political stage. That is the US now and in five years. Maybe not for reasons you think, nor like, nor appreciate, nor agree with, but too bad. They didn't ask you, and it is less and less in your power to get involved in any of it in a meaningful way.

If this is my vision and position, that five years hence marks the beginning of recovery in the US, I must offer core reasons supporting the argument. What will be the catalysts to this change? Indeed, as a falling euro would make me want to take my true love to Europe for the month, a falling dollar makes me want to choose the US instead. In five years the US$ index will be sitting in a new-low range of 60–70.

The argument that a further weakened dollar will cause inflation doesn't matter because there is inflation on the Asia-Pacific side as well. Inflation is inflation for every-one and it is nothing new. There will be wild asset-swings along the way but as the dollar falls, foreign interest and money will roll in on a broad scale. The trend is already in place and now I move the romantic argument of where I can have my cheapest holiday to the business front, sharing the story of the InvestAmerica event that recently took place here in Shanghai at the Grand Hyatt in Pudong.

This world, a world most Americans don't spend time thinking about, is the world of "invest in America." Amen to that. Amen to the Chinese who are so filthy rich with cash that a tour group of 50 needs four hours to make it through customs because every one of them is carrying a bag of cash they need to declare—cash that, by the way, is mostly likely uncounted in China's GDP figures. Amen to the rich Chinese who can easily invest US$500,000–1,000,000 in the EB-5 investment visa residence program. Do you think they are investing in Malaysia, where they can get a green card by investing only US$35,000? Of course not—they want the US, because they love and want many of the things that are great about it.

One Rises, Other Declines

It is not farfetched to recognize the rise of one region of the world balancing the decline of another. This is expected in the course of longer-term economic and social cycles. Let me tell you bluntly: Even as the US has her problems, to any Chinese, a US passport or green card is the holy grail of freedom. The word for America in Chinese is *meiguo*, which means beautiful country—and the newly rich Chinese want in.

They see it, and they intend to buy the US piece by piece, ranging from major banks to local houses and stores. They will own more and more of it. As Europeans came in the early 1900s, the Chinese will come in our age. They don't need to cross the border illegally without money as many from Mexico because they have plenty of money. They, the Chinese (and Asians in general), will diversify American society with a rising percentage of Chinese (and other Asians) in the population because in the future the US will be the place to be once again. But in fact, even now the US is already the place to be for the "new" crop of immigrants from rising Asia, led by China. They are thrilled to be capitalizing on the country's problems and have the chance to buy up US assets on the cheap. They expect the US government to start offering more and more legal incentives and breaks to attract more investment; and indeed, that trend is already in place.

If you think Donald Trump getting his breaks to invest in a declining New York City was a big deal, imagine 100,000 Chinese Donald Trumps doing the same thing. Let's note that, according to *Forbes Magazine*'s 2011 list of billionaires, the US leads the world with 413, up from 403 in 2010. China now has 115, but that's up almost 50% from 64 the previous year. At the US$ millionaire level, the number of Chinese millionaire households is reported to be 670,000. But Rupert Hoogewerf (founder of the Hurun Report, China's "rich list") and I agree that those numbers are still off by half, mostly due to the enormous amount of hidden wealth in greater China.

The other significance of the point is that the vast majority are newly wealthy and have the "conquer the world" attitude that goes with new wealth. So then, some have asked, why would they invest in the US? For two reasons, both strong and intertwined: because they are pragmatic opportunists who love a bargain, and because they still see all the advantages and great things about us through a romantic eye, even with the current issues upon us. They keenly have their eye on the US—trust me; believe me; they do.

They see China's problems—all the rottenness of their country—just as clearly as many Americans see the rottenness of theirs. Thus they have a very high level of interest in diversification, to protect themselves via such measures and establish life, business, and investment across the Pacific in the US. Be thankful for the economic power that the rise of Asia, led by China, will bring to the country's shores in the coming years, in her time of need; her need to recover from an unprecedented—and yes, shameful—debt hangover. The next five years will be rough but will gradually also build the foundational trends over the next five years leading to rebuilding, restructuring, and new opportunities that will emerge. This incoming wave to the US also applies at the academic level. Who are the high-scoring students in college? The Asians, of course. Where do they want to study more than anywhere else? The US.

Is the verdict then "bye-bye world?" No, it's "Asia saves the day as the dollar falls to attractive levels." Five years from now, today's declining US is well on the road to recovery due to the continuing trend of a falling dollar with rising inflow of interest and investment. Doomsday for the US? Nonsense. Never. Ridiculous. All assets, economies, and systems are far too intertwined. By the way, much the same for the state of affairs in Europe; it's a declining situation for many, but the euro isn't going to dissolve.

The Very Bad News

The very bad news is that before meaningful recovery begins in the US, encouraged by a falling dollar with rising incoming foreign interest and investment, the decline is already in place and it is falling squarely on the American middle class right now. It is infuriating, and it is shameful; over the next five years, the decline will continue. Products and services around them will continue to become more expensive, while opportunities to improve life and career will continue to decline. The jump across the canyon to the more secure side of the society will grow wider and wider.

The solution for those in the wrong place at the wrong time—for anyone who does not have money but has a sufficiently entrepreneurial spirit combined with desperate need, is to focus on how to sell anything to the people who do have the money, including the incoming Chinese. This is why all of us remind Washington to beef up the National Exports Initiative program, purposely focus on exports to greater China, build up new manufacturing sector, and create jobs. That's a genuine by-the-book solution.

The trick will be to identify the more secure upper-middle- and upper-income people who are doing the buying; to find out what they need and want; and to do your darnedest to position yourself to sell it to them. Since your job prospects are miserable, you may as well give it a go, including partnering up in small groups to form small companies, opening stores on Amazon, Alibaba, Taobao, etc. Identify what the incoming Asian money is investing in and figure out a business plan—a project to offer them to do business with you.

This does not help the many middle-class folks who are not inclined toward, or capable of, moving forward. For the group of 50–100 million lower- and middle-class Americans who are truly stuck, the budget retail industry will flourish, supported by government programs, continuously expanding food stamps and other social support programs, so that they can at least get by. Walgreen's 2-for-1s and Filiberto's fresh-but-really-cheap burritos mark the budget lifestyle.

This aspect marks the rise of the lower-income Asian lifestyle in America by necessity: families sharing residences, renting out rooms, eating basic, low-cost meals consisting of noodles, rice, meat, beans, veggies. Second cars will continue to decrease in numbers while bicycle and scooter counts will rise. Merchant thinking will rise and small, cheap-to-open local stores and flea markets will pop up, like the shop-houses of Latin America and Asia. As covered here earlier, more will go to gardens, fresher and cheaper, for food. Meanwhile, taxes for the rich must and will rise.

The US is becoming a completely different place than it was, marked by the decline of the middle class, making the next five years amongst the worst in American economic history for that strata of the country. Yet, as for the rest of the population and society, if one can imagine that vivid separation and marginalization, they will continue to thrive, with plenty of wealth and job security to weather the economic storms to come.

Food and Oil Can't Go Much Higher

Meanwhile, what's the outlook on the equity and economic side of the picture over the next five years? The S&P will rollercoaster but end up close to where it is now, if not 20% higher. Same for the Hong Kong and China indices. Interest rates will rise, but not by much—and so will oil, because the world economy cannot withstand oil at too high a price. Agricultural commodities have peaked now and won't go higher for the next five years. These items won't be higher because they CAN'T go higher. The gold/silver complex will continue to rise toward those US$2,000/US$100 targets or more. The Chinese yuan will still not be a free-floating trading currency.

The rich elite are greedy but not so stupid as to ruin it for themselves. So, to return to a statement I made many months earlier: In the face of a potentially higher US$, US treasury and other bond yields worldwide, pieces of the sovereign debt, pensions, Social Security, and other fixed income assets will be somehow set aside, forgiven, defaulted, dissolved off the books, renamed, re-categorized, hidden, re-classified, or adjusted with more mark-to-market type shenanigans. They'll make new choices and new policy announcements as needed to keep the global economic system going and avert "disaster."

Mrs. Yan Kicks Butt

Let's humanize this. My pregnant wife asked me 30 minutes ago to go out and get her the local egg pancake breakfast she likes from her favorite street vendor, Mrs. Yan. We live a one-minute stroll to the nearby subway line in a lovely, older local neighborhood. As volumes of people stream to the subway, street vendors have their portable breakfast carts out—think New York hot dog stands, only much older and dirtier with big, rusty crooked wheels. Mrs. Yan looks to you and me from a Western point of view as a hard-working street person: frumpy, unkempt, worn down, and uneducated. She is all of the above; she probably can't even write Chinese.

Mrs. Yan kicks ass. She has done it every day for perhaps the past fifteen years. She serves up 200 of her one-minute fast, fresh pancake/egg-crepe things from her coal-fired stovetop on wheels every morning at RMB 3 (US$0.46) each. Her costs, my wife and I calculate, are less than US$0.15 per unit. She repeats this feat in the afternoon. So our frumpy Mrs. Yan has been earning US$120 per day, every day, seven days a week for countless years. Add it up; that's US$3,600 per month in cash. She is far richer than most living in her 70-square-meter apartment with her husband, who was probably an engineer earning US$300 per month for the past 20 years.

With monthly expenses of around US$600, Mr. and Mrs. Yan have socked away US$360,000 in ten years. Mrs. Yan hides her cart in the apartment garden behind the gate at 9 a.m. because that's when the police come on duty and might otherwise come and take her stuff because she is running an unlicensed business. In some places the police are more vigilant about preventing unlicensed businesses and street vendors, for the simple reason that they don't pay any taxes. This is reasonable if the taxes are reasonable, which they are. But in cities of 10–15 million people, this way of merchant street life continues to thrive.

Now, wash, rinse, and repeat millions of times across China and other emerging market countries where the merchant lifestyle is the root of the lower/middle class and invisible cash is king. Now do you understand? Should you even bother to note reported GDP figures from

China? This is what the US moved away from. On top of that, manufacturing went away, which, compounded with the banking shenanigans and bad governance, spells big trouble for the country. Into this big trouble will come some—note the word "some"—of Mrs. Yan's US$360,000 in cash, because she just wants to give herself and her children options—not perfect options, but reasonable options and choices—ones that are now open to her as our valuations decline.

Now raise the scale of this to the new, far-richer Chinese people and companies who are doing the same thing, looking to spread their wealth, give themselves options, and expand their investment opportunities across the globe. Like any good business person. I don't think we should all read too much more into it.

Let's not forget the story starts with Mrs. Yan churning out US$0.40 egg-crepe things, like a little factory day-in and day-out, keeping her mouth shut and doing her thing. Dear Mrs. Yan, the nice, local, foreigner guy with the pregnant wife is writing about you in a book that will reach across the globe, discussing some of the most critical issues and trends of the socio-political and economic landscape. What a world.

How Can This Be

Here are some questions or rebuttals some readers have had:

Mario, what happens to your views if (or when) the dollar loses reserve currency status?

Well, that would certainly change everything for everyone and we all know that. Right now 80% of international transactions take place in US$.

Why the heck would the Chinese want to leave their form of overt communism to come here for our "more restrictive form of communism?"

That question assumes so much! The simplest answer I can give you is the famous "The grass is always greener on the other side of the fence." Many are so damn blinded by the miserable, annoying stuff going on in the US that you are not capable of seeing how anyone else anywhere else on the planet can find opportunity or benefit from what is happening.

Let me tell you very clearly what I see and what Chinese see from here in Shanghai. We see two countries, both with lots of pluses and lots of minuses, and both being completely different sets of pluses and minuses!

So, let me have access to both—that's reasonable—and let me decide how to live my life in either place. We want options. Especially the Chinese, more free and capable than ever to gallivant around the globe with their cash.

The Chinese spy on their citizens.

Oh, come on, stop whining. In the US they also spy on citizens through email, phone, cameras on the streets. But is it really a big deal? I heard that in Scottsdale, the citizens moaned so much that the city actually removed the speeding ticket cameras from the 101 freeway!

I can't believe it. Here, cameras are built into the system on every single block of road, snapping photos of the cars as they drive along. I gave up on the idea of the supposed privacy and freedom Americans idealistically hold up. It hardly exists anywhere on earth, not there and certainly not here, so move on. You can still probably have a nice life where no one will come knocking on your door if you're not doing anything nefarious.

Yes, I know that it's not fair that they screwed everyone and took away your ability to do anything about it. I know, I know, it sucks; we can go on and on about it. I am not ignoring it nor saying it isn't a big deal, or isn't very important or aggravating. It is all of those things. But now what? What matters now is what we notice—and how we respond.

No Pollyanna

The scenarios I have laid out have been referred to as gentle or rosy or Pollyanna-ish. Heck, I also wrote a substantial section about how there is a huge, ugly price to pay in what is happening; that that price is being paid dearly by one of the largest, most important and influential group of people in the world to now, the American lower and middle class. I wrote that, and there's nothing rosy about it.

Remember—the Chinese conduct business quietly, the more under the radar and quieter the better. They are silently rich, have silently saved for a rainy day for years beyond belief, and that rainy day is here right now, isn't it? On any day anywhere in the world, the one with the money is the one with the upper hand, an easy reality to understand, as much as its implications create concern, doubt, or even furor.

I have decided this is the greatest lesson I could share if you would share a lesson:

Chinese do business the way they drive cars: Pragmatically, unpredictably, and unemotionally. That is, many of them (the male drivers, for the most part), drive like maniacs: Cutting each other off, swerving lanes, and not staying in the lanes. Yet no one gets upset (because in this society there are side-of-the-road vehicles all over the place—scooters, work-carts, bicycles, big buses) and so swerving out of the white line is necessary and so normal to them. It is pragmatic action; it is emotionless; they rarely get upset.

They are patient. They virtually ignore each other's crazy driving. There is almost zero politeness, the idea of courtesy is exception, not rule; yet again, they don't regard each other as rude at all. They simply recognize that you and I are equal in our task to get from point A to point B, we are both concerned only with ourselves, and we are both trying to get where we need to get—so why should either of us be upset?

At the grocery store, clerks don't say hello or thank you to a customer. They just ring up the stuff; that's their job. There is no expectation of anything else in terms of a social interaction; it's all incredibly pragmatic and process oriented. So consider what all that might mean as the rise of Asia, led by China, impacts the rest of the world. It is quite a culture clash.

By no means should anyone, including myself, imply that this part of the global economic picture is a broad-reaching panacea or solution to the many woes the world faces, woes faced by the Americas, Europe, Asia . . . everyone. But it should be considered a very meaningful part of what is happening in the current and coming state of world affairs, and I believe we should all keep it in mind.

Of Common Mind

Yes, China definitely has a collectivist mentality, but recent years have seen a blossoming of more and more individual freedom and opportunity than ever before. Beijing is in a precarious position of allowing a blossoming civil society yet fears what may happen if it gets too out of hand, and it's become even tougher for them with the expansion of the Internet and social media. They allow far more open expression of public opinion now; for example, you can see article headlines in magazines about gays and lesbians in China, articles about the promotion of new bishops in the Catholic Church, articles about China's many problems, and reality shows copying those in the West. All of these flourish in the mass media and Chinese web more than ever before. So while America has gone too extreme in the direction of individualism, China had been too extreme to collectivism and is moving aggressively toward the middle.

For this reason I have to take issue with some of the extremes some Americans suggest in their descriptions of China and collectivism. Chinese society is better than ever in allowing and creating individual opportunity. This cannot be refuted. The people heading out there aren't missionaries, they're just individuals trying to expand and improve their lives.

That said, the rules are still strict. From what you might have seen of Chinese news, when an upper supervisor gets caught making a mistake in regard to tainted milk, lead in children's toys, or whatever the business scandal of the week may be, he is executed. It wasn't a mistake, it was pure greed and bribery, and when a leader does it and gets caught, he's done. If you have perpetrated damage against our society, it's bye-bye to you.

In China, everyone knows these rules. It's like Singapore. Don't throw gum in the street; if you get caught, pay five hundred dollars. Vandalize a car, get caned. Remember that story a few years back? You know the rules, extreme as they are. This gives us a clear understanding of why, along with the lack of guns, crime is so low in China.

Crisis or Circus? (August 2011)

In the daily give-and-take of the Rick's Picks *forum, Mario Cavolo, an American expatriate living in Shanghai, is the perennial optimist, sort of. While hardly unmindful of America's steep decline, he sees offsets in a rising global middle class, particularly in India and China, and in an upper-class America that will continue to flourish even in hard times. Skeptical though we are sometimes about his thesis, we must admit that a drive through Palm Beach, Florida, the other day reminded us that there are concentrations of wealth in this country so deep that even if 90% of it were to vanish tomorrow, the super-rich will still be driving Bentleys and shopping on Worth Avenue and Rodeo Drive. For a summation of Mario's thoughts as US stocks continue their descent into hell, read on.*

—Rick Ackerman

Let's begin this commentary by asking exactly what specific Lehman-type crisis recently occurred or will occur to justify the nasty global equities decline and its continuation as what may come to be known as the 2011–12 Crisis? We can quickly dismiss the idea that it was Standard & Poor's credit downgrade of US debt. I mean, come on folks, it has been beyond obvious that global credit markets are awash in debt and therefore higher-risk. Things were known to be bad before the downgrade, and the downgrade itself did not make the fundamental problems any worse. The credit downgrade was a message to Washington, one long overdue, but it probably did more to soil S&P's reputation than it hurt the US, since nobody has forgotten that the firm rated sub-prime junk as triple-A a few years back. So let's move on to more substantive issues to identify what is wrong with the global economy right now.

Can we say it was a recent "realization" that Washington bankers and politicians have been greedily pillaging the financial system? No, the reality of those issues has been baked into the cake forever. We are far beyond any hope that those in power—I hesitate to call them leaders—in Washington or on Wall Street will do the right thing. Neither bankers nor politicians are ever going take a bullet for the good of the country. Rich people just don't do that sort of thing, reminding us why a wise Biblical figure named Jesus quipped one day about it being easier for a camel to pass through the eye of a needle than for a rich man to enter heaven. Indeed. They will, however, adhere to the values of any seaworthy captain—and go down with the ship.

Wildly Overvalued?

Moving on to the withdrawal of Bernanke's QE, should this be expected to cause a fresh crisis of sorts, and if so, why? Have publicly held companies performed so poorly lately that the stock market has become wildly overvalued? Hmm, that's a tough sell. How about the fact that interest rates are likely to remain near zero indefinitely? Doesn't that support the flow of money into riskier assets like stocks?

In fact, doesn't a stock portfolio of reasonably priced, financially sound, dividend-paying companies—MLPs, REITs, and other such vehicles—sound like a superbly good idea right about now? Isn't it true that global companies like P&G, Yum! Brands, and hundreds of others will, by the nature of their economic position across the globe, have their shares priced in balance with any currency fluctuations and inflation?

If not any of the above issues, then it must be those trillions of US dollars being pumped into the system, right? Nonsense, I say! What's a few trillion dollars amongst crooks and the citizens of the world? More money in circulation means inflation of goods and services. It does not necessarily mean hyperinflation.

The sharply reduced purchasing power of the US$ and other currencies across the past four decades is nothing new, as so many intelligent analysts have pointed out, and we have confirmation that it will continue along with global expansion. Now let's rise up and argue that "we" can't afford higher prices. But we must stop and ask who is this "we"?

A Nation of Renters

Now let's turn to the US real estate debacle. Yes, this is really horrible: 100 million lower- and middle-income families of America are ruined, including being upside-down in their homes and moving toward becoming a rental society. But this group of people is NOT THE END-ALL, BE-ALL OF the world economy, or even the US economy! There are another 150 million Americans whose lives are stable and good, and they are wealthier than ever. They have high-paying jobs, their kids are in college, the companies they work for are not going out of business anytime soon. Am I wrong about this?

It's easy to understand why Americans and Europeans living in the US and Europe narrowly see doomsday with all of its related horrors. After all, the closer you are to the pain of others, the worse it seems and the more of it you feel. However, need we be reminded that the world is not composed only of a declining US middle and lower class? I think this pain, this very real pain, has caused a terrible distortion in the American view of the state of global affairs.

View from Shanghai

From my vantage point here in Shanghai, I'm reminded that the lives of 150 million Americans are better than ever, that stock valuations are not outrageous, that the rise of Asia, led by China and the other BRIC countries, is a long-term, multi-decade reality as was the rise of post-WWII America; that the global tech and web-driven shifts transforming the world are individually and together powerful trends with the potential to more than offset the shameful shenanigans of Washington and Wall Street elites who have disgraced the word "leaders." Make no mistake, the biggest problem in the US today is its dismal and corrupt leadership—of government, financial, defense, insurance, lobbying, and legal sectors.

The country's second-biggest problem is that it is confused about its identity. It doesn't know that it is no longer "The Greatest Nation on Earth" any more. This is where the true and sad delusion lies. (Read *Give Me Liberty* by Naomi Wolf for an insightful understanding of this.) Even adding in Europe's similar sovereign-debt excesses, that still doesn't sound a doomsday siren for the whole planet.

Because the US economy, its financial and political system have broken down to varying degrees doesn't mean it's the end for all of us. Those billions who are poor have always struggled, and so there is not so much change for them, even as a rising middle class in China, India, and elsewhere more than offsets a declining middle class in America. That does not make the struggling, angry American feel better, however, nor should it.

What the American middle class needs to do is summon to action the spirit that made the US great to begin with. Although broad socio-economic changes will be playing out globally in the years ahead, the situation is reasonably described as a period of unprecedented social, economic, and technology-driven shifts and transformations. But I readily acknowledge that this positive, expansive picture that I present is being threatened by one of the most disgraceful periods in American political and financial history, and a leadership unprepared to face the truth.

Who's to Blame for the Death of the American Middle Class? (October 2012)

We occasionally publish guest editorials with which we disagree, but seldom have we disagreed more vehemently than we do with the praise the author has heaped on Ben Bernanke—a mountebank in our book—for supposedly doing his job well. Fortunately, it is not Bernanke that is the main subject of this essay, but rather, corporate greed and its role in impoverishing the American middle class. The writer is Shanghai entrepreneur and jazz pianist Mario Cavolo, an American expatriate and Rick's Picks *forum regular who usually manages to see the bright side of a darkening global economic picture without being a Pollyanna.*

—Rick Ackerman

Ben Bernanke is the only person who is doing the right thing at the right time under the right circumstances. Let's thank him for doing the only thing he can do to save the slowing world economy. I have decided to print up 10,000 "We Love You Ben" stickers. Even better, let's go with "Ben's Got the Balls We Need—Because No One Else Does."

Rather than blame "Helicopter Ben" like everyone else, let's ask ourselves what's really going on. What is the bottom-line problem for the average American? Yes, start reading between the lines, because the masterful spin doctors and populist media-driven messaging are more deceptive and manipulative than ever. They've mastered the art of getting you to look in all the wrong places for all the wrong reasons. If you were in Ben's position, wouldn't you be offering the world billions in easing rather than letting the economic edifice collapse, creating global havoc, and spreading social unrest?

Shall we compromise and say that you would do some parts the same and some parts differently, but no matter what, you would have a supportive, accommodating, monetary policy if you were in his position? Let's hope so, because while letting everything collapse and fail sounds good in a local bar chitchat or some world economic forum, in reality it would be devastating. You think 8% unemployment, 20% underemployment, and 50 million on food stamps is bad? Try 30% unemployment, 100 million on food stamps, and the associated descent into social chaos—which is where we would probably be right now if the unsupported S&P were back at the ominous 666 figure. To blame Bernanke and friends for the problems of today is to be ignorant and naive. It is too easy, too pat, and I implore you not think like populists and the mainstream media.

For now, let's set that issue aside and instead ask, "What is the real problem, the one that most directly impacts the typical lower- or middle-class American, the heartland citizen of the country?" The answer is that the people who are in charge, truly responsible for the good of the US, are not doing what they are supposed to be doing. Is Ben your city's mayor? Is he your state representative who's supposed to be representing your interests and needs in Washington? Is he the boss at your company?

It's time to turn off the TV, stop reading newspapers and web-based news, and start looking closer to home, the place where most Americans stare into the face of their biggest problem. I think you will be surprised to find how easily we can identify the real culprits and how accessible they are. And in fact, the solution doesn't require any government involvement at all. Don't jump to conclusions as to who they are, and don't jump ahead of me. Let's first look at some blame-game favorites so that, by process of elimination, we can identify the real culprits.

Target #1: Blame "the Wealthy"

Historically true. The wealthy actually do run the show and make the rules to favor themselves. This past decade has given us the greatest wealth-grab ever. Is this something new in history? No, it is not. And while it seems a convincing way to explain away the issues of the day, and while it does relate to the real problem, let's move on to issues less vague and which speak more directly to the real problem in the American society and economy with a solution with more impact that even a five-year-old can understand.

Target #2: Politicians

True—and pathetic. Abraham Lincoln is rolling in his grave. "Of the people, by the people, for the people" has been relegated to the trash heap of political and leadership irrelevance. Let me not bore you with what you already know: The self-serving greed and corruption that causes you as a citizen of America to wince in disgust as you turn your gaze toward the world of politics. Obama's presidential re-election campaign raised over US$180 million in September alone. How do we describe, without harsh criticism, a political system that has gone so far out of control and away from its sense of responsibility to its country? Once again, as appalled as we are and should be, this is a separate world, like Mars, and not a direct part of the root problem the typical American family faces.

Target #3: The Decline of Social Values

Sadly, this one is true. As the third generation of an Italian-American immigrant family, I am appalled and saddened by what we have become. The deterioration and transformation of marriage and family values are a central contributor. While there are other cultural forces at work that we can discuss with respect to the deterioration of societal values, let me strongly suggest that the destruction of traditional marriage and family has made America one of the most emotionally dysfunctional and behaviorally twisted places in the world to live.

In the majority of cases, the emotional devastation to a child from a divorce, especially a typical US-style divorce in the American court and counseling system, has a much broader, negative impact on society than most care to admit or acknowledge because, frankly, it is just too painful. I can already feel the divided, rising anger of rationalizations on the subject. For example, in today's Catholic church,

I know of typical cases where a young couple informs a parish priest they want to get married in the church, and the response is far from the encouraging, happy talk the naive couple is expecting.

In fact, the priest will often hang his head in disgust and ask with sarcasm, "Why would you want to do THAT?" already knowing that the couple haven't a clue what a true marriage before God is and what they are undertaking. Admonitions to *not* take your vows unless you truly mean them and intend to live their vocation are heard, but not comprehended. How can they be when you live in a society surrounded by divorced people and your own parents are divorced? The Catholic Church is keenly aware it has been fighting a losing battle in this regard. Alas, this is a subject with far-reaching implications for further scrutiny by sociologists and theologians alike, but analyzing it still only leads us further down the path to the real problem.

Target #4: Blame China and Related Globalization

Now we're getting closer. As a person who has lived in China for thirteen years, in a marriage to a traditional northern Chinese wife with a one-year-old and mother-in-law, I have often been a critic of the anti-China bias that distorts people's view of the many issues related to China. Ranging from supposed censorship vs. supposed freedom, to supposedly "freeing" Tibet (whatever that means), to communism vs. democracy vs. socialist market capitalism (huh?), the mud-hurling never stops. In this arena of issues, the two things we know for sure are that big business sold out the US middle class to cheap labor overseas and likewise sold away its technology.

Now we see the rise of Asia, led by China: the ones with all the cash coming back to the US to save the day by, for example, snapping up post-financial-crash real estate bargains. They are laughing all the way to the bank, and the big lie out of China is not that they are exaggerating the stats to show things are better than they really are, but that they are in fact quietly hiding how well they actually are doing. Many a book has been written on China-related issues, most of them, especially by the populist doomsayer authors, getting it completely wrong, misguiding one into believing a false reality. As we find this subject has overseas cheap labor at its core, I will hint that it is closer to the real problem. Let's see what it is.

The Real Problem: Corporate Greed and Stagnating Wages

The real problem is simple and in your face. Are you surprised we're not blaming something or someone that has to do with the government? What, Bernanke doesn't sign your paycheck? Isn't it great that S&P 500 company profits are at record highs? Doesn't it make you feel more secure about having a job? But have you noticed anything odd about your paycheck over the past couple of decades, especially the past four years since the 2008 financial crisis?

Do you spend money that you don't have at the end of the month? If you did have more money at the end of the month, wouldn't that money make its way economically into society? If you had more, wouldn't you spend more? Of course you would.

Wouldn't having more of the money you deserve and have earned stimulate spending, investment, and then wouldn't productivity go up due to increased demand from your spending and investment? The average American's problem is corporate greed in the face of record profits and hoarding of cash. You need to talk to the boss if you want a raise, a raise you deserve, have earned and they can easily afford to give you, and there lies the problem.

Yes, I love you, Ben Bernanke, for covering and protecting the losses of the greedy banking sector so that the economic system does not collapse. However, my more direct problem is my paycheck and the source of that problem lies squarely in the private sector, the company I work for. So then, why has the government been so easy on its demands to the private sector, starting with the banking industry, while making US taxpayers bear the burden?

For example, I've always wondered why Bernanke doesn't offer to match rather than just give? "We'll put up if you also put up." Sounds like a nice policy to me! Wouldn't it make a lot of sense if Ben said, "Yes, we'll pledge US$50 billion per month to cover the national bank's bad debts and, at the same time, corporate America will stop hoarding its trillions, which by the way is against the interests of the shareholders, and agree to match that by releasing US$50 billion per month more in wages to its employees."

We'll do our part as everyone else does their part too, working together for the good of the country. That is a powerful combination that will get the American economy humming again. We'll provide quantitative easing, but require that the companies make commitments too, that they will start distributing those record-breaking profits and hoards of cash to their employees who are way overdue for salary increases, and stop paying their executives millions of dollars in annual compensation. On these obvious and fair requirements, Washington has been silent. But this does not stop American workers from gathering together to address this issue with their bosses in the private sector.

Servitude

Yes, of course those financial/banking excesses shouldn't have been allowed to happen in the first place, which all started with the repeal of Glass-Steagall. But far too much attention has been spent focusing on this popular American blame game. We are not focusing on that problem here. The US economy needs more money in the pockets of the middle class who are the primary spenders and consumers. Instead, they are being slowly choked to death financially, choked into corporate employee servitude.

American corporations are experiencing record profits and sitting on record levels of cash—a stockpile in excess of two trillion dollars. Where's yours? Where is your share of that? Why did your boss decide to stop fairly distributing those profits into employee paychecks? That's the core problem, and it's not political.

While myriad expenses and costs of living have been going up all around you, your wage has withered in the cold wind. So stop blaming Bernanke; stop blaming Obama; stop blaming Washington; stop blaming the politicians. They are not your boss; you can't go to them and say, "This company is hoarding its profits, we want a raise!" They don't dictate the size of your paycheck. They are not the ones running your company. They aren't the ones hoarding the cash and failing to raise your wages appropriately for the past several years. While the other problems cited here are far from simple and there is plenty to criticize, I'm thinking a few thousand employees need to head to the next shareholder meeting and start making a fuss where it counts.

In China, there is a dearth of qualified workers amongst the multinational companies. That is why wages have been steadily rising and loyalty is low. In the US, if the qualified, experienced workers rose up together in protest, would the company be able to replace them? What excuse does your boss have for his or her sinfully high salary while your own wage doesn't even keep up with the rising cost of living? Why are Americans taking this state of affairs like a flock of beaten-down sheep? Money needs to trickle back down into the economy to stimulate the economy. I suddenly have a new respect for the idea of unions to try and help solve this issue without overdoing it. What about the power of the shareholders of these companies to do something about this obvious problem? This problem is the real problem, not a sideshow or related issue, because unlike the others, it is the issue that most directly touches and impacts Americans in their daily lives.

Behind the Shell Game Lurks a Black Swan (October 2009)

When we half-jokingly talk about "DaBoyz" and how they are continually manipulating the markets, we sometimes lose sight of the fact that they really are out there, rigging the game so that they cannot lose. However, even as these Masters of the Universe maintain quasi-criminal control over the short- and intermediate-term swings, they understand, as we do, that there are larger, uncontrollable forces lurking in the form of black swans such as the collapse of Lehman Brothers. A post in this forum from Mario Cavolo brilliantly describes the interplay between the manipulators and those larger, dangerous forces. Here's Mario with some thoughts on the subject that hit us like a bolt of lightning.

—Rick Ackerman

I have been in a state of particularly deep pondering of these issues for the past few days, stimulated by the way, by my carrying around and reading Nassim Taleb's classic, *Fooled by Randomness*, from which I gained a sudden insight. In the same way that I have learned here from you and others as well, we realize that "DaBoyz," the "Plunge Protection Team" and various other interested groups, such as the Goldman Sachs trading desk, with such ability, even possibly illegal ability, interfered and manipulated the market with enormous cash infusions after the March low, forcing it up beyond reason and fundamentals, such heavy-handed manipulations demonstrated by all kinds of evidence in daily trading activity and volume spikes.

"They" Have Decided

Well, guess what? "They" are at it again, my friends, and why shouldn't it be the case? In the short- and intermediate-term time frames, they absolutely can and do manipulate index levels, gold, and the dollar if they want—right or wrong? Those same "Boyz" have made their latest set of new strategy decisions, of what will go up or down in the range they've decided, within the context of the current overall state of affairs and the intermediate-term time frame.

The action, including strange inexplicable things, is sending the message right now:

- Yes, gold and stocks have had their nice ride to the topside of the trading range, and there is not much upside left IN THIS INTERMEDIATE TIME FRAME, so it is time to take profits, let the market breathe, correct, and trade sideways. "They" KNOW that's what most everyone IS thinking now: there is very little upside to this run and few are foolish enough to take that risk. "DaBoyz" know it too, and know it's time to let it breathe and correct for a while. Reading Taleb taught me about this "asymmetry" in the upside and downside.
- Yes, at the same time as stocks/gold are popping up, the dollar has had its scary ride down to the lower side of its trading range and now it's time to take those stock and gold profits and park it safely in dollars.

Adjust and Pray

A dangerous game? Yes, of course. Do they have a choice? No. They have to do this, to address it, to manage it, to make choices, (while also preserving their own status, of course). They are responding and adjusting, responding and adjusting, while praying that some random black swan doesn't suddenly appear again to disrupt the delicate balance of the sand pile currently in place. The state of affairs here in October is quite different than in May. In fact, what would you really do to unwind it, to solve it, to balance it, to save it?

I am surely incapable of properly answering such an enormous question.

Will a Weak Dollar Do Us Any Good? (February 2011)

All hell broke loose on this forum after Mario Cavolo, an unapologetic optimist who tends to see the glass as three-quarters full, let fly with the rosiest pronouncements we've heard so far on a US dollar that has been sinking in value for nearly ten years. "So okay then," wrote Mario. "We'll devalue the dollar and a few years later, when US assets are more and more attractively cheap, the money and investment and growth will start to flow back in." This was just too much for Robert Moore. Below is Robert's response.

—Rick Ackerman

How exactly does a weakening currency result in more attractive domestic prices? Or, are you suggesting that as the currency weakens that it will mean stronger US exports, and therefore greater domestic growth? If so, then how, exactly, will these miraculous exports be manufactured?

The cynic in me says that the US will have to hit a very deep and rocky bottom before manufacturing and the ability to export the surplus ever returns to these shores. Our manufacturing infrastructure is decomposing, our labor rate to productivity ratios are the most god-awful on the entire planet (they are now even worse than the UK's, and that is really saying something), and, as Wisconsin demonstrates, the people in this country still seem to feel that they are entitled to a six-figure gross income in exchange for doing manual labor that requires no more than two hundred hours of vocational school training to qualify for.

We are a long way from Mario's utopian renaissance. However, I do agree that at some point, the "genius" target of Mario's man-crush [Ben Bernanke] will succeed in devaluing the dollar past a heretofore unknown/unseen inflection point where foreign dollar holders, no longer able to trade dollars for oil or local currencies, will instead repatriate these dollars back onto US shores. The result will not be real growth in the US economy or increasing real incomes for American citizens. The result will be unreal nominal growth in US prices.

I firmly contend that the global repudiation of the dollar, which is just now getting under way, will end up yielding a domestic repudiation of the dollar within the next five to ten years. There are simply too many dollars in global supply for this not to come to pass. I know you are all thinking, "but what about the Fed soaking the excess supply back up by raising interest rates?" Really? Look what a measly 125 basis-point increase in the prime lending rate did to our housing market in 2007.

What do you think a real increase of 500–800 basis points will do to our economy? Now consider what a Paul Vockerian 1,000–2,000 basis point increase would do. I don't think I even have to mention what a 5% increase would do to the ability of the government to service our existing debt, not to mention all the new debt that emerges from year-over-year budget deficits.

Dollar Is Finished

Here's a hint: It wouldn't stimulate our manufacturing and exporting machine, that's for damn sure. Simply put, the dollar is finished as a valid measure of qualified economic capital. Finished. The game is over, even though there still seem to be a lot of players on the field thinking that if they pick up the ball and run for the goal that they will make a difference on the scoreboard.

Basic, incontrovertible economic facts:

- *The dollar is a measurement of debt; therefore the supply of dollars indicates the supply of unpaid debt.*
- *All debts must either be paid in full, or defaulted on. The US money masters can only have one real goal in mind, and that is to keep the dollar on life support long enough for the Chinese real estate market to implode, and for Chinese price inflation to hammer the underprivileged hard enough for the "Egyptian effect" to hit Shanghai.*

I am convinced that there is a metric. I don't know if it is a preconceived dollar level on the US Dollar index, or if it is some level of backwardation in the Gold market, but I do know that when that metric (whatever it is) is reached, there will be a statement by Bernanke (that is probably already prepared) to Congress where he makes the soft "observation" that Gold "seems" to be acting more like a global currency than simply as an input commodity to the jewelry industry. And that will be quite a day.

—Robert Moore

Mario's Response

An engineer can tell us at what point a specific material will break when holding x amount of load; a doctor can tell someone (approximately) how long they have to live when inflicted with a deadly disease. The way I see it, this can go on almost forever. I have friends (many of them) whose lifestyles haven't change a bit; they are oblivious to the problems that the other 80% are having. They're planning expensive vacations, they're paying for expensive schools for their kids, they're golfing all the time on "business" trips, their wives don't work and just go shopping, on and on.

It is completely confounding to me. I don't get it.

Ackerman Weighs In

End of argument, really, and you've made the point beautifully: Foreign investment in the US implies a lower standard of living for most Americans.

—Rick Ackerman

This is such an important point, perhaps summarized also as to say that a falling dollar is not going to help the lower-/middle-income class Americans who are being hurt the most by the changes and shenanigans that have been and continue to take place; those whose circumstances are in decline face a huge fundamental socio-economic shift.

Except to say, out of the hellish ashes of change do come some opportunity; as entrepreneurs they could somehow get involved in new growing business opportunities in the US, of which the exporting sector is one, and selling stuff to the rich incoming foreigners with money being the other.

About the Author

October 2013 marks Mario Cavolo's fourteenth year living in China. He is the Vice President of Scott PR China public relations agency, a professional speaker, communications advisor and media event personality. Mario is the Project Founder of the QT2 Wellness Project, a health & wellness initiative in collaboration with corporations and restaurant/nightlife partners providing QT2 e-cigarettes to alleviate the problem of China's 350 million smokers who smoke a staggering 5 billion cigarettes per day. In 2012, Mario was invited to be a facilitator for GE's Professional Leadership Development programs, and as a visiting lecturer on communication messaging and delivery at top ranked CEIBS MBA school.

Mario's client engagements with Fortune 500 and Chinese companies include CBRE, Dow Chemical, KONE, AEGON-CNOOC, Solvay, eBay, PayPal, Siemens, American Airlines, PPG, Alcatel-Lucent, Qiagen, and many more. He has appeared on Bloomberg television sharing his views on the growth of China's economy.

On the artistic side, Mario is an accomplished jazz pianist with China Art Hangzhou Agency, performing his repertoire of jazz and international standards in concert several times per year throughout greater China. Derived from his first book, *Catalysts To Change*, he frequently incorporates piano performance and creative concepts into keynote speeches. Mario, his wife Nana Zhang, and son Vincent reside in Shanghai.